Day by Day with God

May–August 2003

DAY BY DAY
WITH GOD

Bible Readings for Women

MAY–AUGUST 2003

Christina Press
BRF
Tunbridge Wells/Oxford

Copyright © 2003 Christina Press and BRF

The Bible Reading Fellowship,
First Floor, Elsfield Hall, 15–17 Elsfield Way, Oxford OX2 8FG

First published in Great Britain 2003

ISBN 1 84101 200 9

Jacket design: JAC Design for Print, Crowborough

Trade representation in UK:
Lion Publishing plc, Mayfield House, 256 Banbury Road
Oxford OX2 7DH

Distributed in Australia by:
Willow Connection, PO Box 288, Brookvale, NSW 2100.
Tel: 02 9948 3957; Fax: 02 9948 8153;
E-mail: info@willowconnection.com.au

Distributed in New Zealand by:
Scripture Union Wholesale, PO Box 760, Wellington
Tel: 04 385 0421; Fax: 04 384 3990; E-mail: suwholesale@clear.net.nz

Distributed in South Africa by:
Struik Book Distributors, PO Box 193, Maitland 7405
Tel: 021 551 5900; Fax: 021 551 1124; E-mail: enquiries@struik.co.za

Acknowledgments

Printed in Great Britain by Bookmarque, Croydon

Contents

6   The Editor writes...

8   Contributors

10   A Morning Prayer

11   Prayer   1–10 May
      Sandra Wheatley

21   Genesis   11–24 May
      Wendy Pritchard

35   1 Corinthians 13—16   25 May–7 June
      Anne Coomes

49   The gift of music   8–14 June
      Elizabeth Rundle

56   2 Chronicles 10—20   15–28 June
      Rosemary Green

71   Through the valley   29 June–5 July
      Ann Warren

78   Holiness   6–19 July
      Chris Leonard

92   Psalm 37   20–26 July
      Beryl Adamsbaum

99   Message to the seven churches   27 July–9 August
      Alie Stibbe

113   Coping with upheaval   10–16 August
      Christine Platt

120   Romans 5—11   17–31 August
      Diana Archer

135   Magazine section

156   Order forms

158   Subscription information

The Editor writes...

It always surprises me the way words can jump out of the page at you when you are flipping through a book or a magazine, and that is often just enough to give you an idea about the publication and whether you want to read it thoroughly. I have just done this with *Day by Day with God* and the words that I kept noting were 'peace' and 'be still'. Perhaps we only pick out what we need to see—another person doing the same with this issue might find a very different selection.

We are secure

Diana Archer is continuing to lead us through Romans, and she wonders if we, as women, find it difficult to accept that we are secure as God's children without having to *do* anything else, possibly because we can rarely say we have finished everything that 'needs to be done' in our everyday life. Perhaps this is why the words 'peace' and 'be still' came to my attention—as I need to learn how to be still before God without being distracted by all the things I feel I must do *today*. Beryl Adamsbaum writes notes based on Psalm 37, and it was her heading 'Be still' that caught my attention: 'Be still before the Lord, and wait patiently for him' (v. 7) is perhaps a verse that I need to write on the top of my 'jobs to be done today' list. It is only too easy to let the business of each day crowd out time to be still before the Lord.

Coping with change

Since *Day by Day with God* began, back in 1998, there have been many changes in the circumstances of our contributors. Many of our readers will also know what it is like to cope with change. Sometimes these changes in our lives give us happiness and renewed enthusiasm in all we do; other changes can be catastrophic and cause great sorrow. Chris Platt, one of our writers in this issue, has recently emigrated to the other side of the world and this has prompted her to look at incidents in the Bible where people have had to deal with change in their lives. How they trusted God in all their varied circumstances. Another contributor, Ann Warren, has written about walking through the valley of the shadow of death when her husband Peter was diagnosed with incurable cancer.

Perhaps the change that tests our faith most is losing someone we love—when we have to learn to trust God with the present and the future.

I trust that this issue of *Day by Day with God* will help keep us secure in the knowledge that God loves us and is with us whatever each day brings.

Mary Reid

Dr Ann England

Day by Day with God is the result of the vision originating with Ann and Edward England, of Christina Press: they saw the need for notes written by women for women. Ann wrote, in the introduction of the first issue in 1998, that the 'aim is to help us walk closely with God and to know how much we are loved and valued by him'.

After a long illness Ann finally went to be with her Lord in June 2002. We will miss her wise contributions to *Day by Day with God*.

Ann worked for some years as a doctor in obstetrics and gynae-cology at Manorom, the Overseas Missionary Fellowship hospital in central Thailand. She then married Edward and with him was joint publisher of Christina Press. For some years she was also a trustee of Burrswood, a Christian centre for healing. John Perry, the Bishop of Chelmsford, described Ann as 'a person full of grace and the Holy Spirit'.

Before her illness Ann wrote notes based on Jeremiah, ending with the question, 'Why did God send his Son?' and pointing us to the answer in John's Gospel (3:16): 'For God so loved the world that he gave his one and only Son that whoever believes in him shall not perish but have eternal life'. Ann's life and work were dedicated to both physical and spiritual healing—passing on to others this good news of the gift of eternal life.

Contributors

Beryl Adamsbaum is a language teacher living in France. She is involved in teaching, preaching and counselling and writes short devotional articles.

Diana Archer is a writer and editor, and has three teenage children. Starting a church in her lounge with her husband Graham, an Anglican vicar, led to her writing *Who'd Plant a Church?* (Christina Press), a warts-and-all account of church and vicarage life. She now works with the Damaris Trust in Southampton, producing Connect Bible studies.

Fiona Barnard lives in Scotland. Her principal work is among international students, encouraging local churches to reach out in friendship to those temporarily far from home.

Anne Coomes has been a journalist for the Church of England for nearly twenty years. Together with the well-known artist Taffy Davies, she has launched www.parishpump.co.uk, a website providing articles for parish magazine editors. Anne also does freelance communications work for various dioceses, and has written five books. She holds a degree in theology and is Reader for her parish in north Cheshire.

Rosemary Green has left the staff of Wycliffe Hall, Oxford, in order to have more time for ten grandchildren and for her local parish. She continues to be involved with *Women in Mission*, and she loves writing for BRF, trying to make the Bible alive and relevant in a world that is increasingly ignorant of this book.

Chris Leonard, her husband and two student-age children live in Surrey. Chris has a degree in English and theology and her twelve books range from biography and devotional to children's stories. She enjoys leading creative writing workshops because 'people are so interesting—and they grow!' Recent BRF publications include *The Heart of Christmas* and *The Road to Easter* (co-written with Jacqui Gardner).

Christine Platt worked for ten years with The Navigators, living in Ivory Coast and travelling widely throughout Africa. She has written booklets, articles and the SU *Lifebuilder* study book on 'Forgiveness'. She now lives in New Zealand.

Wendy Pritchard is the wife of John, Bishop of Jarrow. She is a learning support assistant at a church secondary school, and mother of two daughters—one now married. Wendy has enjoyed each different phase of her life, from vicar's wife and maths teacher to mass caterer. She is interested in gardening, computing and solving life's problems.

Elizabeth Rundle is a Methodist minister. Most of her life haas been spent in Cornwall, and she and her husband were married for 21 years before he died in 1988. Her book *You're Never Alone* has been written to offer hope to those who are bereaved. She has also written five books of daily readings, led pilgrimages to the Holy Land, and contributed to religious programmes on radio and television.

Alie Stibbe has a degree in natural sciences and spent five years in medical research before beginning to write for *Renewal* and other Christian magazines. Alie is a postgraduate student in the Department of Scandinavian Studies at University College, London. She is married to an Anglican minister and they have four young children.

Ann Warren started her career in the BBC as scriptwriter and producer and has written a number of Christian books. She is a trained counsellor, and was a regular contributor to the television programme *Company* and, more recently, a *Christian Viewpoint* speaker. Ann and her husband Peter spent many years working overseas and she has three married daughters and three grandchildren.

Sandra Wheatley lives in County Durham, is a qualified nurse and was diagnosed with multiple sclerosis fifteen years ago. She is single, lives alone, but is not lonely as family and friends live nearby. She has a variety of interests which keep her actively involved in the lives of those around her.

**Contributors are identified by their initials
at the bottom of each page.**

A Morning Prayer

Thank you, heavenly Father,
for this new day.
Be with me now
in all I do
and think
and say,
that it will be to your glory.

Amen

Most

Prayer

For this reason, ever since I heard about your faith in the Lord Jesus... I have not stopped giving thanks for you remembering you in my prayers.

Prayer fascinates and mystifies me; it forms the structure of most of my days. It is the vehicle I use to meet with God. My response to him. But what is it? If someone were to ask you, 'What is prayer?' What would your answer be? I asked lots of friends that question recently. Their responses spoke of dependency on God; communion; friendship; worship; practising the presence of God... and much more.

In the classic book *Prayer* by O. Hallesby one definition of prayer is, 'the breath of the soul, the organ by which we receive Christ into our parched and withered hearts'. 'The breath of the soul...' Breathing is something we do without thinking or planning—we don't have to tell our bodies to inhale and exhale, it just happens. Such are the wonderful mechanisms in these bodies of ours. Just recently even this simplest of tasks has proved to be a problem for me. The muscles in my chest have succumbed to the MS too, pain and spasms catch my breath so that I am often conscious of each breath I take and aware that it hurts to breathe. The mysteries of MS! It is teaching me not to take even the simplest things for granted—I'm aware of breathing and how important it is to continue. I am also aware of the importance of prayer as the breath of my soul... the life it brings and the Life it brings me into contact with.

This verse begins with 'For this reason...' We know we have a very good reason to breath but how important is it that we pray? To catch a glimpse of prayer as the breath of the soul gives us a wonderful reason to continue.

Dear Father, we have many reasons to pray—for help, for others, for communion with you. May prayer be as simple as breathing to each of us today. Amen.

SW

The privilege of prayer

Devote yourselves to prayer, being watchful and thankful.
And pray for us too...

Paul's letters are full of encouragement to pray for one another and requests for his friends to pray for him. It is such a privilege to pray for one another—whenever someone asks me to pray for, or with, them my heart is thrilled. But why should praying for others be different from talking or listening to their cares and concerns? What makes prayer so different and such a privilege?

The answer may be in whom we go to rather than what we say or anything we can do. The privilege is twofold. To draw alongside someone else, to listen and to enter into their lives isn't something I'd ever take for granted—or do lightly. The privilege is in the permission to be there, side by side with another soul in need. To then take that life to God in prayer can be one of the greatest expressions of love we can give. Praying for people enables you to love them more and more. Sometimes praying for my friends reminds me of the time Jesus washed the disciples' feet—it is an act of service.

The other aspect of the privilege is to Whom we pray. We come to him not because we must—but because we may. He is the only one who hears and answers prayer. We don't need to formulate the right sort of prayer using the right tones and language—he hears what we say and how we say it. He meets with us in prayer and meets our needs through prayer.

What a privilege to pray for others—and a privilege to pray to Jesus. In being devoted to him we can then be devoted in this most wonderful way of speaking and being with him.

'What a Friend we have in Jesus all our sins and grief to bear. What a privilege to carry everything to God in prayer.' Thank you Father. Amen.

J.M. SCRIVEN (C. 1855)

SW

Reliance on prayer

One day Jesus was praying in a certain place. When he had finished one of his disciples said to him, 'Lord teach us to pray...'

The Gospels give us many instances of Jesus praying, he prayed in secret, he prayed in times of spiritual conflict. He prayed all night before he chose the 12 disciples. He prayed on the cross. He was reliant on prayer. No wonder when the disciples witnessed him praying they asked, 'Lord, teach us to pray'.

What followed was 'The Lord's Prayer'—Jesus' blueprint for our prayers. As his followers do we still ask him to teach us to pray? Do we follow his example in being totally reliant on prayer? Is the Lord's Prayer something we know by heart; does it burn each day within our hearts as we come to him as 'Our Father in heaven...' Do we base our prayer on the awe of hallowing his name—or shift awkwardly because it seems so long since the last time we came to him. Do we feel awkward—or are we in awe?

Prayer isn't only for the desperate and despondent. It isn't only the cry of the helpless and the hopeless. It is our communion, our line of communication with God. Throughout the Gospels we read of Jesus taking and making time to pray, he was in constant communion with the Father. His prayers show us his dependency upon God the Father and his need for time alone with God.

The Lord's Prayer is the simplest of prayers. If you are struggling to pray, can't think of the right words or feel more awkward than in awe, please take some time to read through it again and again... even if you feel you know it by heart... let it be your beginning again to commune with God through the very special words Jesus gave to us. Join with him and enjoy your time together.

Take some time just now to pray the Lord's Prayer and know that it is your prayer too.

SW

Answered prayer

... they called on the Lord and he answered them...

I am convinced that there is always an answer to prayer. We often expect a 'yes' from the Lord in response to our prayers. We are distressed when the answer seems to be 'no' and downright depressed when it is 'not yet' and dismayed when, worse still, there is silence.

Is silence an answer? It is certainly the most difficult to deal with. Someone once said, 'the absence of evidence isn't evidence of absence'. God is constantly at work on our behalf, we simply aren't aware of it most of the time. The apparent absence of an answer to our prayers doesn't mean that there isn't one.

A little while ago a friend's dad developed a serious illness that initially defied diagnosis and treatment. His condition worsened and our prayers increased. After months of concerted prayer—and believing—he died. My friend was devastated.

Some weeks later she phoned again. Her car had developed a fault and the garage was having problems fixing it. I joined her in praying. Within a matter of hours the fault was found and the car was fixed. I couldn't help but wonder why the car was fixed after prayer and her dad died... we prayed together, we believed together. Both were answered prayers. I'm sure that you will have instances similar to those and have similar questions to mine.

We often think prayer changes things—I feel that prayer changes me—often the 'things' I am praying for stay the same. We are not responsible for the answers—that is the Lord's business. The part we can play is to pray—that is all the Lord asks of us. It is he who answers.

Prayer takes us beyond our demands and needs and ushers us into fellowship and friendship with God. He does answer—directly, indirectly; obviously or shrouded in mystery. Whichever way, we are promised the answers will come.

Heavenly Father, may we accept whatever answers to our prayers you grant us today—and always. Amen.

                                                                    SW

Yielding prayer

*'My Father, if it is possible, may this cup be taken from me.
Yet not as I will, but as you will.'*

Jesus' prayer in Gethsemane is the starkest example of a yielding prayer. Few of us will ever reach the extremes Jesus did. Not only was he to give his life for us, but he was to take upon himself the sins of the world. We may never fully understand it, all we can do is accept it.

In this modern age how evident is yielding? It seems such an old-fashioned word these days, especially as we embrace our human rights. We yield to no one. One definition I came across says yielding is 'to surrender, relinquish, to give way, to comply'. All attributes of the Christian life and yet yielding prayer is one of the most difficult prayers we will ever pray.

I have struggled recently to pray a yielding prayer. But with his infinite patience the Lord has allowed me to come to that place of seeing yielding not as a negative, harsh thing, but as the next step along the path he has planned for me. It isn't *giving in*, rather *giving up* my life in compliance to his will and raising my hands in surrender to him.

I use a wheelchair, what I can't do for myself it does for me. It gives me mobility. I no longer walk—I ride! In essence, when I sit in it I *yield* to it. I have learned to use it, to accept it as my means of mobility. When I yield to the Lord in prayer it is in recognition that he can take me, he can move me, he can do with me what I cannot do for myself. I yield to his will. I give to him what I cannot keep and receive from him what I cannot lose.

Dear Father, I yield my will and my life to you. I surrender to you and your glorious will for me today and every day. Amen.

SW

Philippians 1:3–4 (NIV)

Enjoyment of prayer

*I thank God every time I remember you. In all of my prayers for
all of you I always pray with joy...*

Paul's epistles ooze with joyful exuberant prayers—he obviously
prayed with joy and encourages us to do the same. So why is it for
many a difficult and sometimes guilt-giving discipline rather than an
anxiety-relieving practice? What has changed from a privilege to an
obligation where it becomes arduous and lengthy, where we feel to
have accomplished anything in prayer we have to plead and beg and
long and wait?

There are seasons of experience where prayer is a challenge and
the heavens do seem 'as brass'—but can it still be possible, even at
those times to enjoy praying?

If an aspect of prayer is friendship with God, and I believe it is,
then wouldn't it be far more enjoyable if we were to see our times of
prayer as we would see visiting or speaking with our closest friend.
When I meet with friends we usually launch straight into talking,
sharing, laughing; sometimes crying. There are times of listening
and even silences. It is good to be with my friends.

When I meet with God I tell him all that is on my heart—even
though I know he knows my thoughts and words before I utter
them. Sometimes there are silences. Sometimes I am aware that his
presence is so close I could reach out and touch him. It is good to
be with my God.

I even chatter away to God all day long as he has 'escaped' the
confines of my quiet times. Keith Green wrote a song which began
'Make my life a prayer to you...' That is how I want to live—not in
a traditional musty old prayer, but with joy alongside—that is communion, that is friendship with God.

---

*Dear Father, make my life a prayer to you today and may I know the
joy of friendship and communion with you all day long! Amen.*

SW

Resting prayer

He makes me lie down in green pastures, he leads me beside quiet waters, he restores my soul…

Resting or restorative prayer—how we need to know how to rest in these days.

Is there such a thing as 'resting prayer' or is it a whim of mine? We have taken a very brief look at some aspects of prayer that may have been helpful. I've steered clear of the more weighty aspects of prayer that others have written about and have brought great encouragement—and challenge.

My experience of prayer has moved through many phases, I struggled and wrestled with God in prayer. I've battled and interceded on behalf of others and I've discovered the wonderful truth that prayer isn't a magical set of words or phrases that move God into action—it is my means of contact and communion with him.

In these days of fraught and frantic activity we need a place of prayer where we can lie down beside still waters and know the refreshment and restoration being with him brings. The literal translation of 'pray always' is 'come to rest'.

I have a confession to make—I sometimes fall asleep when I pray. It has been known that when I close the day in prayer with my friend Jan that I fall asleep when she prays. I've even fallen asleep while I have been praying! Am I the only one? I hope not. Usually resting prayer involves little activity, few words, all that is needed is a response to him and a recognition that nothing is required of us except to 'be' in his presence.

Resting prayer is possible; is needful if we are to engage in those aspects of prayer that take us to the front line in the battle for the souls around us. May you find not only rest for your weary and battered life but a place of resting prayer where he can restore your soul and meet with you as you are.

Jesus says, 'Come to me… and you will find rest'. He's waiting for you.

SW

Prayer of Hannah

In bitterness of soul Hannah wept much and prayed to the Lord...

This is one of the first recorded 'prayers' of a woman in the Bible—
there are many instances of people speaking with the Lord—mainly
men—but this is the first time a woman is spoken of as praying.
Hannah was to be the mother of the prophet Samuel.

She was married to a man called Elkanah—he had another wife,
Peninnah. Hannah was childless and was taunted by Peninnah
because she had children and Hannah didn't. Elkanah didn't help
matters by saying, 'Don't I mean more to you than ten sons?'
Whether this was the final straw for Hannah we aren't told. But she
went to the central sanctuary with Elkanah and prayed her prayer
of desperation for a son. With the prayer came a vow to give the
child back to God all the days of his life.

Her prayer was answered and the prophet Samuel was born.

Hannah wasn't the first and will be by no means the last woman
to pray for a child. Her prayer was born of desperation and 'bitterness of soul', she did not know what else to do except to come to
God and pray.

Your situation may be the same as Hannah's, you may even have
a husband like Elkanah who feels they are more than sufficient to
meet all your needs. Your circumstances may be very different but
your desperation the same. All you can do, all that is best to do, is
pray. Sometimes the prayers we pray out of desperation are our most
effective. We don't have time or the inclination to formulate the
right words. From the depths of our beings we cry out to God.

God will see to it that the answer will come and something wonderful will be born into your life!

---

*Dear Father, when we are in despair or desperation may your ear be
attentive to the cry of our hearts. Amen.*

SW

A woman alone

There was also a prophetess, Anna... She never left the temple
but worshipped night and day, fasting and praying.

Anna was 84 years old. She had been a widow for most of those years, and now spent her days and nights fasting and praying—devoted to God and like Simeon spoken of in the previous verses, waiting for the appearance of the Messiah. We know little else about Anna—yet she was to be the first person to proclaim that the Messiah had come.

Anna and Hannah shared the same name—it apparently means 'gracious'. Hannah was certainly gracious in her life with Elkanah. Hannah came to the temple—Anna stayed at the temple. They both had something and someone very special to praise God for.

Anna's devotion to God can be matched by few of us. Life and circumstance can sweep us along leaving little time to spend with God. For those who are married the demands and delights of a husband and children leave little time and space to 'worship night and day' as Anna did. That is why I feel very privileged to have the luxury of time. Being single and living alone I can and do pray—sometimes during the night. I realize that for many of my married friends their lives—wonderful and fulfilled though they are—have so many other demands placed on them. Yet I see lives just as devoted, just as touched by God as they meet with him. I've realized that 'time' isn't just a question of minutes or hours spent in his presence—it can be an attitude and momentary glance into the face of God in response to him. Thank God he doesn't measure our commitment or devotion by any other means than our heart's response to his calling.

Dear Father, whether we have the luxury of time today or are pulled
in so many directions by family commitments, hear our prayers and
feel our response to you. Amen.

                                                              SW

The Lord's Prayer

*My prayer is not for them [the disciples] alone. I pray also for
those who will believe in me through their message...*

Jesus left us a wonderful example and blueprint for our prayers when
he taught the disciples to pray (Luke 11). We know through the
Gospel writers that he was often in prayer but not many of the
prayers have been recorded. This is one of his last.

To read John 17 is like eavesdropping on a conversation between
Jesus and God and here in this verse is a reference to you—and to
me. Can you believe it—Jesus is praying for you and for me! We are
those who have come to faith through the message the first disciples
and apostles preached. Two thousand years ago Jesus prayed for you.
And it didn't stop there—Hebrews 7:25 says he is still interceding
for us.

There is something comforting and encouraging in knowing that
our family and friends are praying for us. There are times when I
know that someone, somewhere is praying for me and I get such a
boost from realizing that. That Someone is quite probably Jesus. It
is also such a thrill when I feel a particular 'nudge' from the Lord to
pray for someone too.

Few of us are totally alone but some are and have no friends or
family who know them well enough to pray for them—that thought
saddens me as I know the richness of friendship and family care and
prayer. Jesus has promised never to leave or forsake us and here is
his prayer, in this intercession for us is evidence of his love for us.
Even before we came into existence. Take heart and be encouraged,
not only are you seen by God—you are being prayed for right at this
moment by his Son.

---

*Heavenly Father, thank you for Jesus' example of his life of prayer.
Help me to follow on—to pray for my family and friends day by day.
Amen.*

                                                                sw

Genesis 1:1–3 (NRSV)

Light out of darkness

In the beginning when God created the heavens and the earth, the earth was a formless void and darkness covered the face of the deep, while a wind from God swept over the face of the waters. Then God said, 'Let there be light'; and there was light.

Genesis draws together the old stories of the Jewish people. These opening verses paint a vivid picture of the beginnings of time, recording the story of God's creative love—a reminder of his hand in the past, and a reassurance of his continued care. This is a picture story, with layers of meaning, not a literal attempt to explain the origins of the world scientifically. Whether the world was created by a big bang, or a process we have yet to discover, God was in it. He loved the world into being, and works with science as much as poetry. The God who was pictured moving over the face of the water, bringing light out of darkness, is a God of power and wholeness, bringing order out of chaos. This is God on a huge scale, no comfortable pocket-sized deity we can confine to Sunday mornings. This God speaks, and it happens.

All too easily we can limit God to the equivalent of an old man with a beard. We go through the motions of prayer, sleep through the sermons, sigh for the state of the world. We need to find again this picture of primeval power, to remember that it is an awesome thing when we say that God is with us.

Through the centuries, God has not lost his ability to bring light into our darkness, whatever shape our own personal gloom may take. Many different circumstances can make the darkness creep up—bereavement, self-doubt, relationship problems, failing health, worry about money or the future. God knows all about the darkness and he wants it put back into its proper place. We need only to offer him the smallest of cracks and his light can flood in. He is a God of power.

Lord, shine in my darkness, especially in .... Bring your light to .... as well.

WP

God's perfect creation

God saw everything that he had made, and indeed,
it was very good.

What do we see, and think it is very good? What makes us smile in appreciation of it being created? Here are a few of my favourites—maybe yours will be here too, or maybe your list will be very different.

The family cat, sitting on my knee while I am typing this, and trying to join in. Our goldfish with veil-like tails swimming lazily and gracefully. A wriggling puppy chewing your finger, unable to contain its excitement about life. Donkeys that will eat off your hand. A robin perched cheekily on the handle of a garden spade. Whales, bigger than I can imagine, eating tiny plankton. Dragonflies skimming the water with shimmering blue-green wings.

Snowdrops and primroses cheerfully braving the weather. Irises with their amazing colouring, roses with their heavy scent. Trees that grow taller than the house, and can live for hundreds of years. Country lanes where the trees meet over the road, forming a green tunnel. The smell of freshly mowed grass. A field of ripe wheat turned to gold in the late evening sun. Boats reflected in the still water of a lake, with shoals of fish swimming silently beneath. The sea crashing onto the shore, with the white clouds racing one another. A clear sky with a myriad of stars, seeing more and more as your eyes get used to the darkness. Snow turning the streets into a Christmas card scene.

A new-born baby, with the tiniest fingers and toes. A six-year-old excited by all the things there are to learn. An athlete giving his all to stretch beyond the boundaries of expectation. An old woman, with wrinkled skin and faltering step, but with laughing eyes and a generous heart. You and me, with all our faults and all our strengths —God loves them all, knows them all, and believes unshakeably that they, and we, are very good.

Try making your own list as you look at the world around you during the day. And remember that God thinks you are 'very good'.

WP

Passing the blame

Then the Lord God said to the woman, 'What is it that you have done?' The woman said, 'The serpent tricked me, and I ate.'

Here we have another very well-known story. Again it is not to be taken literally, and Eve blamed for all the misfortunes of life! However wonderful God may have made life in the story for Adam and Eve, they just couldn't help wanting that little bit more. Surely rules were there to be bent? God would never know. The serpent pushed Eve to eat the fruit of the tree that would make her as knowledgeable as God, and what a temptation that was. The story makes it seem as if Eve didn't need much persuasion, and there was Adam just behind her, letting her take the risk first, just in case it turned out badly. They were together—he could have stopped her—but no, he let her go first then joined right in.

And when God found them, hiding because they now knew they were naked, how disappointed he must have been. He'd given them perfection, but they couldn't be trusted. What's more, they tried to pass the blame, and couldn't even admit their fault and say they were sorry. Does this all sound strangely up to date?

'My work-mate led me on, and he said no one would find out, so I agreed to do it.' 'The neighbours said it was true, and I only passed on what they told me.' 'The other people at the party said it was what everyone did nowadays, so I had to join in.'

We do all have the ability to say 'No', but like Eve and Adam, that requires some self-denial. It also requires an acceptance that God does in fact know what's best for us, and by following his guidance and trying to live by his rules, we will turn out to have had a happier life than if we made up our own rules as we went along.

Is there anything you need to ask God to give you the strength to turn away from? Is there anything you need to face up to, and admit you're sorry?

WP

Beware of jealousy

Then the Lord God said to Cain, 'Where is your brother Abel?'
He said, 'I do not know; am I my brother's keeper?'

After they had left the Garden of Eden, Adam and Eve had two
sons. The firstborn was Cain, who worked the land, and the second
was Abel, who was a shepherd. We are not told much about these
two, but we can guess that Cain felt superior. He was older, tougher
and stronger. They brought offerings to God, to thank him for his
protection of their land and flocks. But as so often in the Bible, God
was drawn to the underdog, the second son, the one who came more
humbly. Cain was furious. He looked down—not up at God to see
that he also was loved, or across at his brother to see the good things
about him—but at his feet in anger. He waited his moment, and in
a quiet field the firstborn son in the human family became the first
murderer.

So now God, who knows exactly what has happened, gives Cain
the opportunity to confess, and Cain blows it. He tries to pretend he
knows nothing about it, and when exiled by God, whines that someone he meets in his wanderings will kill him. Yet God protects even
this spineless murderer, and puts a sign on him to show he is under
God's protection (vv. 11–15).

Now why are we told this story so early on in the Bible? We may
not be tempted to murder as Cain was, but we can all fall prey to
jealousy. We can resent a brother or sister, a more successful col-
league, a prettier neighbour, a 'better Christian'. Jealousy is a fierce
emotion, and it can sweep rational thought aside. We need to do
what Cain didn't or we will be swamped by it—look upwards to
God, and sideways to our brother. We may not be our brother's
keeper, but we can learn to be his admirer. Instead of resentment, we
can train ourselves to look at our neighbour with God's eyes, and
see the good inside.

Help me to affirm my neighbour's strengths, not resent them.

WP

Life and death

Thus all the days of Methuselah were nine hundred and sixty-nine years; and he died.

Our last dog was 'as old as Methuselah'. She was 16, very arthritic and wobbly on her legs, and practically deaf. She liked to be near me and I felt really guilty that I moved around so much—she just got settled and I was off again! But we were used to her ways, and she had shared so much of our history that we almost felt she would live for ever.

Even Methuselah couldn't manage that, though! The way years were reckoned then may have been very different, and the writer used big numbers to show that in these early times the people were close to God's created ideal. Remember that Genesis is telling a story, not competing with the theory of evolution, and although Methuselah lived longer than any other person, death came anyway.

None of us can predict the lengths of our lives, but we can trust God to be with us and those we love when the time comes. I have a friend who was in a very nasty car crash. Her car was heading for a wall, and as she raced towards it she remembers thinking that she was not afraid of death. She woke up in hospital, very badly shaken but not seriously injured, and the memory of that lack of fear has stayed with her. Somehow God was there. A nice image is to think of our lives as walking with God as a friend, so deep in conversation that when we reach the gates of heaven we just step naturally inside. His love will gently guide us in.

But please let us value our older people while we still have them. Sometimes our modern culture of frantic busyness can squeeze out the time needed to appreciate what they have to tell us. They hold our history and our memories—God doesn't see wrinkles! Many saints come wrapped in grey packages.

Think of some older people you know. Try to imagine them through all the stages of their lives, and thank God for them.

WP

Signs of God

I have set my bow in the clouds, and it shall be a sign of the covenant between me and the earth.

In the story of the flood, Noah is saved by God and rescued with his family and pairs of all the animals to start a new life. The rainbow is God's sign that he would sustain the life of the earth, that he has put aside his destructive war-bow (the Hebrew word is the same as for rainbow) and shown his mercy.

In our modern age we tend to be sceptical about signs from God, but he can still break through. My husband was recently consecrated as Bishop of Jarrow. This meant us moving from Canterbury back to the north-east, leaving behind many friends, a beautiful house and garden, the cathedral over our back wall and my teaching job. As we drove towards Durham on the morning of the consecration, feeling rather small and unsure, a magnificent rainbow stretched across the horizon in front of us. We felt as Noah must have done, that this was a sign of God's love and care for us, and that everything was in his hands and would be all right.

But God isn't in the business of covering the skies with rainbows whenever we need them, lovely as that may be. He can show us his love and concern in many different ways. I've just applied for a job teaching a violent student in care, and I know friends were praying about it. The job was withdrawn 'due to unforeseen circumstances', and instead of feeling disappointed I must look on this as God showing that this was not 'my job'. If we ask for God to help, we must then accept the answer.

God's guidance and affirmation may come through a feeling that something is right, through the prompting of a Bible verse, through the wisdom of other people. But we need to have our eyes open to see God in action, and train ourselves to look out for disguised rainbows.

Look today at the world around you, and see its beauty as a sign that God cares deeply for you.

WP

Pride

Then they said, 'Come, let us build ourselves a city, and a tower with its top in the heavens, and let us make a name for ourselves...'

After the flood, you would have thought that the people would have learned their lesson, but no, here they are at it again. Now they've got together and are in the process of building a tower. The Hebrews thought of the sky as the floor of heaven, not very far above the earth, so that a tall enough tower could eventually reach right up to heaven. Then they would be equal with God. You can almost see them—mobile phones in hand—ready to announce to the world that 'man no longer needs God'. In the parable, God then scatters the people and mixes up their language, the only way to halt their boundless ambition.

In our world today we are surrounded by towers trying to reach heaven. Great companies, powerful institutions can thrust upwards seemingly with no reference to God. The poor and the lonely are left out of the picture—speaking a different language and dreaming different dreams. There is nothing wrong with progress—we all benefit from it—but there must be right motives and a clear acknowledgement that we are children of God and not his betters. We need to learn the language of inclusion and care if we are to fashion a tower we can be proud of.

And it's not just big institutions that demonstrate pride. We all have a tendency to think 'Haven't I done that well; aren't I the special one!'—even if we wouldn't say it out loud. God doesn't want us to be cringing personality-less wimps, but he does want us to see that we are not alone in this world—that he is the giver of our gifts and the one who deserves our thanks and praise for what we can achieve. Then when we 'make a name for ourselves' it will be a name worth having.

Think of some of the things you are good at—don't be modest. Now thank God for them.

WP

Wrong decisions

When he was about to enter Egypt, he [Abram] said to his wife Sarai'… 'Say you are my sister, so that it will go well with me because of you, and that my life may be spared on your account.'

Abram had obediently left his home and travelled to the land promised to him by God. But now trouble hit. There was a famine, so Abram journeyed south to Egypt. Here he was scared that his beautiful wife Sarai would prove to be his undoing—he would be killed to get him out of the way so that the Pharaoh could take her into his harem. So he told her to lie, to say she was his sister, then he would be spared and probably given gifts in return for her. It's amazing she ever spoke to him again!

The inevitable happened, but Pharaoh thought he was doing no harm by sweeping her off, until his household was plagued by disease and he realized something was amiss. How could Abram cope with the guilt? Here was God's chosen man, behaving really badly. At least he had the decency to tell the truth when confronted by Pharaoh. I hope he was really ashamed. He had been trapped by cowardice and fear, when he probably knew all along he should have been relying on God to help, instead of trying to lie his way out of trouble.

But Abram learned from this, and grew in stature because of his mistakes. And we too may need to put wrong decisions behind us and go on to what God had in mind for us. Years ago I drove into the side of a stationary milk float while trying to get round it on a crowded road. It was entirely my own fault. I felt utterly stupid and was at first determined never to drive again. I hope I've learned from this, but I had to come to terms with my mistakes, and then put up with the derisive cries of 'Watch out Mum, there's a milk float' from the back of the car!

Have you made some wrong decisions you feel guilty about? Ask God to help you start again.

WP

28

Speaking out

*Suppose there are fifty righteous within the city; will you then
sweep away the place and not forgive it for the fifty righteous who
are in it?... And the Lord said, 'If I find at Sodom fifty righteous
in the city, I will forgive the whole place for their sake.'*

God has just given Abraham and Sarah the wonderful news that the
son they so wanted is on his way. Now God lingers with Abraham to
tell him that he is going to see for himself the cities of Sodom and
Gomorrah, places of great evil and sexual wickedness. It must have
thrilled Abraham that God chose to share his plans with him, but
having just heard about new life Abraham fears he is hearing about
death. His relative Lot and his family lived in Sodom, and God
would surely destroy the city. Abraham seizes the moment, and is
prepared to argue with God for the rights of the minority.

And God really wants to hear Abraham's opinion, wants to see
Abraham standing up for justice. This is the same man who had
made his wife lie for him to avoid trouble, who had skulked in the
background while she had been whisked off to Pharaoh's harem.
Don't let's ever write people off as beyond change! Abraham goes
for it—he haggles with God for the unjust to be saved because of the
presence of a few good people. He doesn't stop until he goes as low
as he dares—just ten good people would be enough, the smallest
size of a synagogue.

Are we as brave? It's so easy to join in, or at least keep silent,
when others are being condemned. 'Surely nobody likes Mrs Jones
any more', 'All politicians are corrupt', 'Young people have no
respect for authority.' It takes courage to stand up for Mrs Jones, the
politicians and the youth. There are much greater issues than these,
of course—poverty, hunger, disease, hatred. Abraham was no fatal-
ist, believing nothing could be done. Don't let us allow ourselves to
be silent either. God wants to hear our voices.

Pray for any situation of injustice you feel powerless to influence.

WP

Don't look back

*But Lot's wife, behind him, looked back, and she became
a pillar of salt.*

As Abraham had suspected, there was nothing good in Sodom to
redeem it. The people there had sunk to the very depths of degra-
dation, trying to rape the messengers of God and ignoring all the
demands of hospitality towards strangers. This was a place devoid of
love and fit only for destruction. The only people worthy of being
saved were Lot's family, and they were being hurried away urgently.

Lot had chosen to live with the worst of the pagans, where even
the most basic rules of decency were ignored. But however awful a
place Sodom was, it was home and difficult to leave. The angels had
to almost drag them away. And Lot's wife couldn't free herself—she
looked back.

Every guide to this barren area has his own idea about which fea-
ture of the desolate landscape inspired the story of Lot's wife. We
will probably never find out what actually happened, but there is a
very important lesson for us here. It is all too easy to be trapped in
our past, and we need to let God wrench us away from it. The past
is important for making us what we are today, but it must not
become a trap that destroys us. I heard recently about a man who
was being confirmed into the church. Asked what had led him to
take this big step, he told how his daughter had committed suicide,
and when his wife heard the awful news, she had a heart attack and
died. This had led him to think seriously about God. Here was a situation where anyone could have been forgiven for dwelling on the
past, but he had used it as a spur to start a new future.

However hard it may seem, yesterday has gone, with all its joys,
sorrows or regrets. With God's help it can enable us to shape a better future, and not destructively dominate our lives.

---

*Hand over to God anything from your past which you feel is lessen-
ing your ability to cope with today.*

WP

Handing the future over

He said, 'Do not lay your hand on the boy or do anything to him;
for now I know that you fear God, since you have not withheld
your son, your only son, from me.'

In this story, God tells Abraham to take Isaac and some firewood,
and journey off to a distant place to make a sacrifice of the boy. Just
in the nick of time, an angel stops Abraham from killing his adored
son, and Abraham finds a ram trapped in the bushes which is to be the
sacrifice instead.

This is the sort of story that can make you give up on the Old
Testament. How could God be so appallingly heartless as to make
Abraham choose between the child he adored and the God he loved
and served? It sounds like God is encouraging child sacrifice, or at
the very least serious abuse of human rights.

But the writer is intending to demonstrate Abraham's faith, not
portray God as a sadist. Abraham's story began with him being told
to leave his home and his past, and journey off to the new land that
God would give him. Now he is being told to hand his future over
to God too. All of God's promises to Abraham were tied up in Isaac,
and now Abraham had to risk all in believing that God would not
abandon them now. This was the supreme test of Abraham's trust in
God. He told the servants that both he and the boy would be back,
and the young Isaac caught the mood and trusted both his father
and his father's God.

No wonder Abraham was the founder of the Jewish nation—this
story demonstrates a faith very few people could match. On a much
lesser scale, are we able to hand our future over to God? Can we
trust him with our job worries, our family crises, our loved ones?
Abraham had to start the journey not knowing how it would end,
but believing in the God who had never let him down.

What most worries you about the future? Pray for God to help you on
the journey.

WP

God's coincidences

Let the girl to whom I say, 'Please offer your jar that I may drink', and who shall say, 'Drink, and I will water your camels'— let her be the one whom you have appointed for your servant Isaac... Before he had finished speaking, there was Rebekah...

We all know of amazing stories of how couples first realized they were meant for one another. There was a student who knew from seeing a girl's photo on the college notice-board that she was his future wife, before they had even met. My parents met at an engagement party, talked all evening and are still together nearly 60 years on. With Rebekah, it was Abraham's servant who had the initial realization that she was the one for the master's son Isaac. He had been sent by Abraham, now near to death, back to the land of Abraham's birth, to choose a wife for Isaac from the god-fearing folk there. He rehearsed to himself the test sentence he would try on likely looking girls, but he only had to use it once. As soon as he started, there was the lovely Rebekah, all he could have hoped for, and a relation of his master too.

Now Rebekah had to make the great step of faith, mirroring that of Abraham, and leave her home and family to follow God to an unknown land. Scary stuff for a young girl, but all worked out well, and Isaac loved her deeply right from the start. It's good to see that the future of Israel depended on the courage of women as well as men!

Abraham's servant had been praying hard for God's help in his task, and before he had finished speaking, there was Rebekah. We may not get answers that quickly, but God is surely active on our behalf. Has anything happened in your past that you felt showed God's guidance? Any of those 'God coincidences' which made you sit up and take notice? What God could do yesterday he can do equally well tomorrow!

Try to pray expectantly, with the assurance that God will be at work.
WP

Family tensions

When the boys grew up, Esau was a skilful hunter, a man of the field, while Jacob was a quiet man, living in tents. Isaac loved Esau, because he was fond of game; but Rebekah loved Jacob.

Isaac and his wife Rebekah had twins. Esau was born first, a redhead with lots of hair, and Jacob was born second. Jacob was to be the father of Joseph, of 'Amazing Technicolor Dreamcoat' fame. But before he became the nice old man of that story, he had a pretty unpleasant youth to go through first. He was jealous of his older brother, and was much cleverer than him, so set about turning the tables on him, and getting the rights of the firstborn. In this he was aided and abetted by his mother Rebekah, who did nothing to promote family togetherness. She encouraged Jacob to deceive his father, whose eyesight was failing, and disguise himself as Esau to get the blessing reserved for the firstborn. Jacob had already got Esau's verbal promise of relinquishing his rights, in return for giving him a good meal when he was very hungry. What a snake Jacob was! Moreover, Esau had married two local girls who were making his parents' lives a misery. So all in all, this was certainly not a happy family.

Take heart all who are in difficult family situations! I used to think that as a clergy family we were expected to be perfect, to set a good example. That was not easy with two children who felt completely at home in the church and saw no good reason for Mum's restrictive policies. Those with teenage children (and teenage starts at about nine) probably know the delights of having to walk separately from the children to avoid their intense embarrassment at being related to this older non-person. No family is without stress, no family is fault-free. For many people, the hardest task of all is coping with their own family. This is perhaps where we most need God's help.

Is there a member of your family who is difficult or more needy? Pray that God will help you cope with them.

WP

God with us

And he [Jacob] dreamed that there was a ladder set up on the earth, the top of it reaching to heaven; and the angels of God were ascending and descending on it... 'Know that I am with you and will keep you wherever you go, and will bring you back to this land; for I will not leave you until I have done what I have promised you.'

Jacob had gone on the run from his furious brother Esau, who had realized how he had been tricked out of his birthright and was out for revenge. Rebekah had given Jacob a cover story to explain his absence to his father—he was off to find a wife from his kinsfolk, more suitable than Esau's local girls. He was facing the unknown without his mother to help, and he was in need of reassurance. Even a scheming trickster needs to grow up sometime.

In the story of the tower of Babel, the people had tried unsuccessfully to build a tower to reach up to heaven and rival God. Now God takes the initiative to show Jacob how it really is. In a dream Jacob sees how earth and heaven are always connected, with God constantly active between the two. This is what Jacob needs to assure him that he is not alone.

This is the first time that Jacob has had a direct experience of God, and again he can't help but do a bit of bargaining. If God will stand by him and keep him safe until he returns home, he'll stay true to God and give him a tenth of everything. That was a pretty safe promise for a penniless wanderer to make, but it turned out to be a big step in Jacob's eventual rehabilitation. God knew what he was about.

The same vision and promise also apply to us. The ladder is still in place, and God isn't going to let us down. Whatever unknown we are facing, he is going to be with us.

When you are anxious, say the words of the promise: 'Know that I am with you and will keep you wherever you go'.

WP

Love for daily use

*If I speak in the tongues of men and of angels,
but have not love...*

This is probably the best-known chapter in the Bible. It is read hundreds of times each year as brides and grooms stand misty-eyed before ministers, thinking noble thoughts about Love. The bride dares to dream that her man will love her like that in the years to come. Patient, kind, never irritable, generous, understanding. Older women in the congregation compare their marriages to this stupendous definition of love, and sigh.

Paul never wrote it with weddings and romance in mind. He wrote it to describe how the people in a local church should love each other.

There. Like a wet towel in the face, isn't it? That this magnificent chapter on love was written for that prosaic, common-or-garden Christian community you know so well, and which drives you crazy at times. If you doubt you and your husband will ever attain this sublime love, you *know* your local church folk will never even attempt it with each other.

And yet Paul's teaching on love was never meant to be brought out just at weddings, to make people feel noble and wistful. Paul was not interested in soothing, 'blessed thoughts'. He was supremely down-to-earth, realistic, and he taught that this sort of love was what God intended for all Christians to show, every day, *even to their fellow Christians!*

Think about it. Chapter 13 follows chapter 12, where Paul is talking to the Corinthians about God's will for enriching their communal life. He urges them to desire spiritual gifts, and then suddenly says: 'And I will show you a still a more excellent way...' Paul is still talking to the local church—trying to inspire them with the vision of how belonging to Christ's body on earth should transform them.

And isn't it interesting to see where he begins—not with hard questions about the humble, unremarkable, quiet folk at your church, but with the 'spiritual superstars' who tend to dazzle...

---

*What have you associated this chapter with in the past?
Read 1 Peter 4:8–10.*

AC

35

Why do they do it?

... I am a noisy gong or clanging cymbal. And if I have prophetic powers, and understand all mysteries and all knowledge, and if I have all faith, so as to remove mountains, but have not love, I am nothing... And if I give away all I have... but have not love, I gain nothing...

This chapter challenges any Christian who is outwardly successful in his or her ministry. So who are the 'spiritual superstars' who shine in your local church firmament?

What about those one or two who are natural leaders of worship—perhaps able to gather the congregation together and get them really praising God?

What about those in your church who seem to have a profound knowledge of Christianity, who can always find things in the Bible (even the minor prophets!), and always have a Christian answer to every ethical problem?

What about those dear souls who have an incredible faith in God's personal care for them? The ones who never panic when you think they should, and infuriate you at times with 'It's in the Lord's hands'?

What about the Christians who support the campaign for abolishing world debt, who refuse expensive holidays and send the money to the Third World instead? Who prefer to use their bicycles instead of their cars, who buy Christmas presents from the Leprosy Mission or Traidcraft, and who drink Café Direct?

What about the Christians you know who are willing to help absolutely anyone?

Christians like these tend to shine out. But Paul is saying, 'Wait—all this is praiseworthy and magnificent, but what is the motivation behind the action? Do these people have love?' Unless these actions come out of love, these Christians, brave, generous and caring though they are, are missing the point of their calling.

In God's eyes, it is the *motivation* which counts.

In 1 Corinthians 8:1 Paul gives the key principle: 'love builds up'. Read 1 John 4:7–12.

AC

Love is an active verb

Love is patient and kind; love is not jealous or boastful; it is not arrogant or rude. Love does not insist on its own way; it is not irritable or resentful; it does not rejoice at wrong, but rejoices in the right. Love bears all things, believes all things, hopes all things, endures all things.

Read those verses through slowly, thinking of relationships down at your local church. Can you think of examples for each description of love, or of examples that fail each description of love? If we can't get along with other Christians where we are, no matter how maddening they can be, what use can we be of God in any wider ministry?

Have you ever noticed that Paul's description of love is all done by using verbs? A loving person will behave in a certain way. She or he will do, or not do, certain things. Have you also noticed that all these verbs are used in the present continuous tense? Think back to French or German lessons at school: present continuous denotes actions which are happening, and which *continue* to happen. These are actions and attitudes which have become *habitual* to the person, ingrained gradually by *constant repetition*.

Patient, kind... not jealous, not boasting... these traits sound so ordinary, almost banal. So humble. Nothing glamorous. But God calls on *everyone* to reflect Christ's love, and only a few of us to positions of renown. We fail him and are unsuccessful as Christians when we are unloving, not when we live quiet, anonymous lives. Paul's words highlight so much of the self-centredness of modern church life. Here there should be no room for asserting our rights, envying others, or treating them boorishly. There should be no room for gossip—especially under the cloak of 'sharing a need for prayer'!

As for bearing, believing, hoping and enduring each other, well, Jesus bears everything we throw at him. He still believes in us, so how can *we* give up on each other?

These verses perfectly describe the character of Jesus; read them again, replacing his name for 'love'.

AC

Only the heart goes on

Love never ends; as for prophecies, they will pass away; as for tongues, they will cease; as for knowledge, it will pass away.

What is wrong with grown-ups? They don't want to keep dolphins in swimming pools (as my 9-year-old neighbour does). They don't want to hold dog-sleepover parties with their friends and friends' dogs (as my 10-year-old goddaughter does). They don't even want (at least not often!) to wear baseball caps, eat popcorn and play computer games all night (as my 12-year-old neighbour does).

I thought of these youngsters when I read Paul's words: 'When I was a child... I thought like a child...; when I became a man, I gave up childish ways.' No one blames a child for being a child. Indeed, we welcome their enthusiasms—how dull life would be without them! But who'd want to stay a child all their lives? Paul says that life as a Christian should also be one of growth to spiritual maturity.

Paul does not blame the Corinthians for having been fascinated by prophecies, tongues and knowledge as they began their Christian walk. All three were and would remain inspiring gifts from God. But Paul is saying that even tongues, prophecy and knowledge, good and God-given as they are, will eventually become either irrelevant or else be swallowed up in the perfection of eternity. Only love never ends.

When some day we meet Jesus face to face, the tongues, prophecy and knowledge will be irrelevant. Here HE IS—in front of you. Your heart's desire. What is there then? Love.

The heartbeat of our relationship with God now is that he knows us, not vice versa. One day we shall also know him. Paul could not wait! The Corinthians majored on tongues, prophecy and knowledge, but Paul focuses on faith, hope and love—the qualities that 'abide'.

My dearest Lord,
Be thou a bright flame before me,
Be thou a guiding star above me,
Be thou a smooth path below me,
Be thou a kindly shepherd behind me,
Today and evermore.

A PRAYER OF ST COLUMBA

AC

Extra RAM for your hard drive

Make love your aim, and earnestly desire the spiritual gifts,
especially that you may prophesy... he who prophesies speaks to
men for their upbuilding and encouragement and edification...

This is a true story: Some years ago the press officer of a senior bishop in the Church of England was a woman. Everything that the bishop said to the nation (and he said a lot!), and every contact that the national media had with him, had to go through her.

On Sundays this woman attended an Anglican church near her home. She asked if she could help contribute to the life of the local church. 'Oh, yes,' came the answer. 'You can pour the teas on Sunday after Matins.'

The senior bishop's press officer was speechless, then graciously agreed. She didn't *mind* pouring tea—she just knew that there was so much *more* she could have given.

Have you ever wanted to 'be of use' at your local church? And made to feel pretty useless? Take heart: the disinterest in you is not from God. Paul makes clear that the Holy Spirit is eager to use you to *your utmost*—so much so that he will top up your abilities—give you the extra RAM needed in your hard drive!

The Holy Spirit is hoping you will ask for the gift of prophecy... an activity not often found on church lists! Paul doesn't mean prophets as in Old Testament prophets. They were unique channels of divine revelation for a specific time in world history. Instead, this New Testament gift is given to strengthen the local church, and is accessible to any member. Michael Green (*To Corinth with Love*, Hodder and Stoughton, 1982, p. 74) defines such New Testament prophecy as: 'a word from the Lord through a member of his body, inspired by his Spirit and given to build up the rest of the body'.

It is beautifully described in Isaiah 50:4–6: 'The Lord God has given me... a tongue... that I may know how to sustain with a word him that is weary. Morning by morning... The Lord God has opened my ear, and I was not rebellious.'

We'll look more at prophecy tomorrow.

Read Proverbs 16:24; 20:15 and 1 Thessalonians 5:11.

AC

Prophesy to help others

He who prophesies is greater than he who speaks in tongues...
so that the church may be edified.

The Holy Spirit (if not your local church) believes in you. He wants to use you to your utmost in your local situation. He wants to equip you by giving you a spiritual gift. Paul advises asking for the gift of prophecy. This is not crazy, though probably it is wisest *not* to tell people you are thinking about becoming a prophet! If it is meant to happen to you, let it happen.

So how does a Christian exercise this gift?

It all begins with simply doing what every Christian should already be doing—spending 'quality' time daily before God. Reading his word and listening to him. Jesus, the true vine, promised that if we abide in him, we shall show forth fruit. This fruit, says Paul, includes the gift of receiving a word from God for others.

Prophecy is not constant access to insider knowledge, where you walk up to people before a church service and announce: 'God told me to tell you...' , and startle them out of their wits. It is never a way for a domineering Christian to manipulate or exercise influence over others! Rather, it is a daily sacrificial offering on your part—making yourself available to God. Becoming so obedient and sensitive to his prompting that the Holy Spirit can use you as a channel to edify and encourage other Christians. Such 'prophecy' must be exercised with great tact, and may range from insight into God's will for a specific situation, or into the application of God's word to the times in which we live.

True prophecy will always be in accord with scripture, will always be submitted for 'verification' (we are to 'test' the spirits) and will always edify. It will leave the person uplifted, not downhearted.

As for tongues, Paul acknowledges their value in personal devotion, but spells out their limitations in helping the local church in public worship. In contrast, the gift of prophecy affirms the Lord's personal commitment to his church, and that he is in the midst of his people.

Read 1 Thessalonians 5:19–21.

AC

Peace and order

As in all the churches of the saints, the women should keep silence in the churches. For they are not permitted to speak...

Do you believe that it is right for women to lead worship, and be ordained to the priesthood? This verse was quoted a lot in the years that the Church of England was struggling over whether to ordain women or not.

First, let's put it in context: in chapter 14 Paul's priority is not women, but on what should happen when a local church assembles for worship. Clearly, things were getting a bit chaotic in the church services of Corinth, and Paul is trying to bring some order into the situation. Corinth was full of mystery-cults, whose 'forms of service' were informal, to say the least. There were often hours of mad gibbering, beating of gongs, ecstatic dancing, and total self-indulgence.

Paul most emphatically did not want this for the Christians at Corinth. The Christian God was rational. Paul wanted order and self-control in all dealings with him.

Paul saw the need to control those with the gift of tongues (two or three at most should speak and be interpreted), those with the gift of prophecy (two or three at most should speak, and their 'word' be tested), and married women in the congregations who talked in church.

It is difficult to use this verse to tell all women everywhere and for all time to keep quiet in church, because in 11:5, Paul has already referred to women praying and prophesying in church, and seemingly approves of it.

Some scholars suggest that it was not the few women who were contributing to the proper worship of the church that Paul was trying to silence, but the many women who came to church and *talked incessantly among themselves*. Such lack of self-discipline was causing disruption in the church. (It causes disruption each month at my local Women's Institute.) You can almost hear Paul shout impatiently: 'Ladies at the back, *please!*'

Read 1 Timothy 2:1–15.

AC

Tidy up

All things should be done decently and in order.

Have you ever lived in a mess? Worked in a chaotic office? You'll know the prevailing, if unspoken attitude: 'Oh well, so what…'

Have you ever stopped to consider that your mess may be more than just a personality preference? Disorganization comes from a lack of self-discipline, and is damaging. It lowers your self-respect, wastes hours of time, and seriously weakens your overall effectiveness.

Have you ever reflected on what a neat and tidy God we have? He likes routine, things in their place, self-restraint. He dislikes dirt, mess and disorganization. If you doubt this, try and think of examples from the Bible where people living in chaos were able to be used by God. Read Deuteronomy—God seems almost obsessive in his concern for their diet, clothing, management of animals, personal hygiene and sanitation. He ordains proper procedures for every area of life.

When Moses led the people out of Egypt, the daily march was strictly organized, and manna arrived at the same time each day. When Nehemiah was set to rebuild the wall of Jerusalem, his methods were a marvel of efficiency, time management and priority-setting. The praiseworthy woman of Proverbs 31 is frightening. This woman has every moment and every aspect of her daily life under control. She plans, organizes, and thus *gets things done*. Try to find one proverb where lack of foresight, catch-as-catch can and dilatoriness are advised. Instead, find admonitions to diligence, forethought and neatness.

In the New Testament, even Jesus displays this tidiness. He heals the man and then chides him, *Now pick up your bed…* (You can almost hear Jesus adding under his breath: 'Don't just leave it there for us to trip over!')

Tidy, organized, in control. Paul here is in line with biblical tradition in urging Christians that 'all things should be done decently and in order'. Then your life will shine with the polish of harmony, beauty—and productivity.

If you are chronically in a mess, find a self-help book on how to get control of your life and space.

AC

42

Who has affected you most?

By the grace of God I am what I am, and his grace toward me was not in vain.

Gopal was born in Kathmandu. His parents, Hindus, died when he was young. He found work as a gardener for a wealthy family. At 14 he met some Christian missionaries to Nepal, and became a Christian. He met the Jesus whom Paul describes so movingly here—the one who died for his sins, who was buried, and who was raised to life on the third day.

Gopal soon realized Jesus was calling him to more than gardening work. For four years he gardened by day, studied by night. Eventually, with the help of the missionaries, he got himself to Bible College in India. In the early 1980s he returned to Kathmandu and founded a church with his wife and two other Christians. He worked tirelessly to preach the gospel and to disciple his young converts. Today his church has over 4,000 members, in Kathmandu as well as in church plants high in the mountains.

As I write these words, I am planning to change the sheets on our spare room bed, and go shopping at the supermarket. Gopal and his wife are coming to stay during their visit to England. Gopal will preach at our morning and evening services on Sunday, sharing stories of all that God is doing for them and through them in Nepal.

'By the grace of God I am what I am...' and 'I worked harder...' Gopal would echo the sentiments of Paul's words with all his heart. Only by the grace of God has he become what he is. Indeed God's grace toward him was not in vain. It released in Gopal, as in Paul, a total commitment with every fibre of his being. Indeed, both Paul and Gopal would argue that if God's grace towards us does not produce such energetic single-mindedness, there is something seriously lacking in our faith.

Reread Paul's magnificent vignette of the gospel in these verses. What response does it stir up in you? To be totally sold out to God, would there have to be changes in your daily life?

Read Philippians 3:7–11.

AC

They think it's all over... but!

If for this life only we have hoped in Christ, we are of all men most to be pitied.

Several years ago, an elderly churchgoer heard a modern sceptical theologian speaking on the radio. He was a brilliant talker, and systemically set about knocking holes in belief in the resurrection of Christ. The old woman listened carefully, and knew of no equally sophisticated arguments to defend her orthodox Christian beliefs. She reasoned further that as he had been allowed air-time on radio, he must know what he was talking about.

After the programme was over, she sat and thought for a while about what he had said. She concluded it must be true. That meant that everything she had hitherto believed about Christianity was unreliable, if not untrue.

She sat up late, thinking out the implications of this. She wrote a short note of explanation, and then committed suicide.

Ever since the first morning of Jesus' resurrection nearly 2,000 years ago, people have been trying to disprove it, to ignore it, or to explain it away. Why? Because if you can take Christ's resurrection out of Christianity, you have brought the whole house down.

Paul was appalled that the Corinthians did not see this. If Christ has not been bodily raised:

1 *Jesus is still dead.* So it's all over for him.
2 *Our preaching is in vain.* What is there to say?
3 *Your faith is in vain.* What is there to believe in?
4 *We are misrepresenting God.* Jesus was not his Son after all.
5 *You are still in your sins.* There's no forgiveness for your guilt, ever.
6 *Those who have fallen asleep in Christ have perished.* So what is the point of anything?

No wonder that after all that, Paul concludes: 'We are of all men most to be pitied.' No wonder the poor, old, confused, woman lost the will to live.

Read 1 Peter 1:3–9.

AC

44

Popular in Hollywood

But in fact Christ has been raised from the dead...

Have you ever noticed how often the theme of resurrection shows up in Hollywood films? Think of ET, Beauty and the Beast, Die Hard, True Lies, Chicken Run, or Gladiator. The hero is in a conflict, fighting seemingly impossible odds, trying to protect those who depend on him (or her!). Then there comes the scene where the baddies win. The hero is seemingly killed off, or put out of action. The characters depending on him are terrified and helpless. The baddies gloat. No one is left to help them—their hero is dead. They feel despair at their bleak, hopeless future.

Then—whoosh! Somehow the hero is restored to life—comes out fighting and victorious, just when the baddies are putting their feet up. The baddies get a nasty shock—there are some more brief violent struggles, and then all is over. The hero has triumphed!

It is such an enormously popular theme in storytelling that it makes me wonder if it isn't written deep into our human psyche—into the very fabric of the universe.

For Paul, Christ being raised from the dead was more exciting than all these films combined. For one thing, it was *real*. These human stories are only an echo of the greatest, most powerful drama ever.

Humanity *was* facing captivity, misery and death. A hero *was* sent among us, he *did* care for us, and he *did* defy the powers of evil on our behalf. He *did* die, and we *did* despair. Then—whoosh—here he is again! The baddies had a very nasty shock indeed—and are fighting desperately. So daily life has now reached that point in the film where the hero is back, triumphant and just finishing off the baddies. Read these verses and you'll see there *are* fights to come. But the outcome for Christ, just like for Bruce Willis, is never in doubt.

Finally, have you noticed that at the end of all these films the hero is seen laughing with his friends, or in love with his girl? When the hero is victorious, the baddies get their come-uppance, and the characters who have been 'freed' by the hero enjoy friendship and/or love, all in a safe, secure place. Heaven on earth?

Read 1 Peter 4:12–13.

AC

You'll be blooming

*But some will ask, 'How are the dead raised? With what
kind of body do they come?' ... What you sow does not
come to life unless it dies... what is sown is perishable,
what is raised is imperishable... it is sown a
physical body, it is raised a spiritual body...*

Have you ever decorated your home with flower seeds? Try it.

Buy different packets at the garden centre, open them up, give
them a good mix, sprinkle them on scraps of paper towel, and lay
them around the house. Dozens of tiny, tiny seeds. Try different
arrangements to show them off in their wonderful dazzling brown,
grey and black glory.

Great decoration, eh? Just hope nobody starts sneezing near
them, or thinks the table needs dusting!

Our physical bodies do us fine here on earth, but aren't fit for use
in heaven. If we are going to be resurrected in Christ, we need also
to be transformed into his likeness. Only Christ-like people will be
suitable for the beauty, colour and harmony of heaven.

Flowers make better displays than seeds, every time. When we
die in Christ, God produces a spiritual body, perfectly suited for
inheriting the kingdom of God.

In these verses, Paul contrasts Jesus and Adam. All humanity
shares in the characteristics of Adam. We are all of flesh, blood and
dust. This is the purpose of God for us for this world. Then the last
Adam, Jesus, himself partook of flesh and blood. He was eventually
put to death and buried. But Jesus' true origin was heaven, and
death could not hold him.

If the fear of death is ever on you, or over one whom you love,
why not seriously buy a packet of seeds and plant them. Especially if
you are trying to explain your Christian hope to children. The miracle of resurrection, of one body dying to be transformed to a glorious body, could not be more plainly demonstrated.

All who belong to Jesus, and bear his image, will also share in his
resurrection.

Read Romans 6:1–10.

                                                              AC

A drama, but not a crisis

This mortal nature must put on immortality... then shall come to pass the saying that is written: 'Death is swallowed up in victory. O death, where is thy victory? O death, where is thy sting?'

In the summer of 1983 my father was walking down the high street in Richmond, Surrey. He had just had some very bad news, and was upset and agitated. Suddenly he had a heart attack. He collapsed on the pavement outside Woolworths. People called an ambulance. He was put on life support systems and rushed off to Roehampton Hospital.

On Roehampton Lane, a few yards from the hospital, the ambulance engine burst into flames. We were told later that a mechanic, to save time, had put a wire over something hot when he should have put it well under it. It started a serious fire.

The ambulance men did what they had to do. In fear of the fire engulfing the entire ambulance, they followed emergency procedure. They shut off the oxygen to Dad, and shut down all the electrical systems in the ambulance.

My father died. At 59 years of age. In a burning ambulance, in front of the hospital.

The incident hit the press, both local and national. Our local newspaper's banner headline ran: 'Man's life could have been saved.' Those were difficult days for my mother and myself, as you might imagine. Yet only one other time in my life have I been so physically conscious of God's love. I felt utterly secure in his presence. We turned to the Bible and prayer to try and make sense of it all. These verses stood out from the page, practically on stalks: *Mortality must put on immortality*.

I knew then that everything was OK. More than OK. Absolutely fine. And from that day to this, I would miss Dad terribly, but I would never feel desolation or despair.

Dad used to enjoy doing things with flare, being different. He liked to be noticed, to make a splash. Perhaps one day in eternity I'll tease him: 'You couldn't just go quietly in an armchair at 90, could you—*you* had to make a dramatic exit!'

Read Romans 8:18–25.

                                                                    AC

Time for the notices

Now concerning the contribution for the saints...

Last Sunday in church our vicar got mixed up. He forgot to give out the notices at the usual slot in the service. He gave an excellent sermon on the sublime call to forsake all to follow Jesus. Then he picked up a slip of paper, frowned and continued: 'Now about the flower festival next week...'

'Huh?' said some in the congregation. Smiles all round.

I thought of that when I read these words of Paul. After the grandeur of his chapters on resurrection and eternity, he suddenly recalls he had practical news to pass on, and can't close his letter just yet. So Paul turns to prosaic matters. Not flower festivals, but finance, manpower, and various 'hellos' from one Christian to another. It is a fascinating peep into the life of the early churches.

For one thing, this chapter reveals a church which is really international. At least five Roman provinces are mentioned: Galatia, Judea, Macedonia, Achaia and Asia. In the few decades since Christ's death, the church had penetrated into European and eastern, Jewish and Arab, Greek and Roman, urban and rural areas.

Those early Christians made the most of the efficiency of the Roman empire. Roman roads radiated throughout the provinces, Roman legions ensured that travel was reasonably safe, an effective postal system was in place, various hostelries dotted the main roads, and Greek was the *lingua franca*. Good roads, fairly safe travel, reliable communications, places to stay, even a single currency—and the early Christians made the most of it in their financial and ministerial commitment to each other. They invented the 'twinning' and overseas support churches so popular today: in this chapter Paul is concerned about the church in Jerusalem, where there was a famine at the time.

True, the early church did not run to direct debits, but ever organized, Paul urged the habit of setting aside a regular amount of money each week. How much? Paul says 'each of you... as he may prosper'—so relative poverty should not prevent planned, systematic giving.

Pray when you give and give when you pray.

AC

Music for healing

Whenever the spirit from God came upon Saul, David would take his harp and play. Then relief would come to Saul, he would feel better.

While on holiday in Dorset, I came across a lovely shop selling cards plus. It was only a small shop but crammed with interesting things which were just that little bit different. I browsed around, picked out my cards, paid for them, and browsed again, for I couldn't leave the shop until the background tape had completed the Mozart clarinet concerto. The music I loved was creating a lighter and contented mood.

Yes, it was a bit of a damp day, but nevertheless, standing listening to the music really made me feel better. I can quite understand how Saul was helped when, in his black moods, the young David was called in to play soothing sounds. Experts today, in many fields, have discovered the benefits of playing music whether it be to unborn infants or when milking herds of cows. Music enhances well-being in humans and animals.

When, as a teenager, I was experiencing the 'hormonal volcanoes', my furies were always eased if I could thump and crash on the piano. (From the neighbours' point of view, thank goodness I didn't have a drum kit!) Music is that miraculous form of communication which transcends language, age, or gender; it touches the heart without a word spoken. Music is also rooted in memory. It may have been that Saul's mother or sister used to sing and play for him in childhood and those lullabies and folk songs from the past cooled his temper.

In chapter 18, it becomes clear that it was quite usual for David to be in Saul's house, playing his harp. Obviously, if it calmed the king, everyone found things easier with David's music in the background.

Try to take some time today to relax with a favourite song or piece of music. Thank God for what it means to you.

ER

New songs

Sing to the Lord a new song; sing to the Lord, all the earth.

There is a story told about a country vicar who was very keen to have good singing in his church. As we are talking about the 1750s, most church music was limited to choral renditions of the psalms, but this vicar had come across some *new* songs. He had heard and obtained copies of some of Charles Wesley's hymns which he was sure his choir would love. He was right—his choir did love these new works but his congregation was outraged! Things reportedly got to such a pitch one Sunday that as the choir struck up their new 'Wesley' hymn, members of the village congregation countered by loudly singing a psalm.

Well, of course, people wouldn't get so heated nowadays... would they? A glimpse at some 'Letters to the Editor' in the religious press makes it painfully obvious that music in church still causes much high blood pressure. If only congregations could accept music as being complementary to worship rather than forcing 'ancient' and 'modern' into competition.

When we look back into the psalms, we find such an exciting array of instruments used to praise God—lyre, harp, cymbals, trumpets, ram's horn, tambourine, strings and flute. What a joyful noise! What spontaneous music to praise our great God.

Isn't it wonderful that there is the gift of music for every generation and for every part of our world. *New* songs flowing out in praise so that whether we are ancient of days, top of the pops, or among those who just like what they know, there is music for everyone.

In 1886, a 32-year-old Baptist minister wrote a hymn for a soloist to sing at a revival meeting in Massachusetts. Then, it was so new, for us it's now old, but the opening lines are timeless: 'I will sing the wondrous story of the Christ who died for me...'

Lord, fill my heart with your music of love.

Read Psalm 145:1–13.

ER

International harmony

I looked and there before me was a great multitude that no one could count, from every nation, people and language... they cried out in a loud voice...

Some years ago, I was thrilled when my period of study in Jerusalem coincided with the Annual International Choir Festival. I was only able to attend one of the evening concerts and hear only three of the choirs, but that one night made a great impression on me.

At the outside venue, the Citadel, the first of the mixed choirs of the evening took to the floodlit stage. They came from Poland and wore suave evening dress. The contrasting selection of classical songs was glorious and they sounded superb. The second choir was totally different. These singers came from a university in the Philippines and performed in smart, casual dress, with the vibrant timbre of youth. Their music, though possibly less polished than the European choir, was infectious by their pure zest for, and love of, singing. The final choir of the evening came from South Africa. This choir performed in their native costume complete with spear and shield. What a pulsating and exciting sound reverberated around the Citadel with their unique harmonies and rhythms. So much hard work and dedication had been put in by each of these choirs and the audience, who also seemed to come from far-flung corners of the world, warmly appreciated their efforts.

As I sat by those ancient walls, myself also far from home, I thought about the three countries represented on the stage. Each has gone through periods of suffering and here were their choirs singing in a city of suffering. Yet, the marvellous fact was that they were present at the festival, overcoming the past with hope, offering their different languages and styles in the unity of music. That week in Jerusalem brought people together of every colour and language—together in song.

Lord, if only the world could sing in perfect harmony...

Read Revelation 22:1–5.

ER

Jesus sings

**When they had sung a hymn, they went out to the
Mount of Olives.**

It was, and still is, the ultimate goal of every Jewish man to celebrate
the Passover feast in Jerusalem. The disciples had walked with Jesus
all the way up from relatively calm Galilee to the thrust and bustle
of the city in full festival mood.

They had shouted their 'Hosannas' along with the crowd as Jesus
rode on a donkey the last couple of miles from Bethany into the city,
they had watched in horror as their Master overturned the money-
changers' tables in the temple and they had listened, perhaps
wearily, to Jesus warning them of the dangers they would face.

This particular Passover had been different somehow. It was a
festival commemorating deliverance from Egypt but Jesus had
added perplexing words, using the symbols of the familiar bread and
wine to represent himself. Then, at the end of the meal, they concluded Passover in the usual way. They sang.

And this opens up a whole new side of Jesus the man. We think
of him teaching, healing, walking, talking, angry, gentle... but not
singing. It is highly probable that we would have recognized many of
the aspects of Jesus' 'Last Supper'. The *Shema*, the Jewish affirmation of faith, the Song of Songs and several psalms are used today at
Passover. Jesus and his followers would have known these by heart
and obviously sang the psalms to age-old settings.

There used to be a musical quiz show on television called *Name
that Tune*, where contestants had to guess a song from as few notes
as possible. It's interesting how words lodge together so much more
easily in our minds when accompanied by music. This, then, has
been the method of worship since the days of Moses and we are part
of that unbroken line of reverent singers!

---

*Lord, I offer my small voice, lost in wonder, love and praise, to be
added to the eternal choirs of heaven.*

Read Psalm 33.

ER

Musical talent

*Then the man who had received one talent came.
'Master,' he said, '… I was afraid and went out
and hid your talent in the ground'.*

The traditional rabbinic style of teaching stimulated a lot of challenging ideas with often stark and uncompromising riddles and parables. Jesus also used parables and, on first reading, this parable of the talents seems rather unfair, but within the context of music, I have found a helpful clarity to the core truth of Jesus' words.

How many adults can look back on dreaded piano lessons and the wretched times of practice when friends were out doing more exciting things? How many people who learned to play an instrument really well but, er, it's been years since they played, and… they've lost their touch! In other words, we are all very good at wasting our talents. Yet God-given talent, maximized by sheer hard work, commitment and *use*, is greatly prized.

Corrie ten Boon wrote how immediately after the second world war, she was in a hall full of refugees The atmosphere was oppressive with hopeless despair and one woman in particular was at the end of her tether. She had lost all her family, her home and her career with the Dresden bombing. But Corrie knew this woman had a rare gift. Gently she encouraged her to sit down at the dreadful old piano, pushed up against the back of the hall and covered in dust. When this poor, depressed refugee sat and began to play the stained keys, everyone in the room turned to listen. Their faces changed as they realized the piano was being played by a brilliant concert pianist. When she finished, Corrie told her never again to say that she had lost everything, because she had God's priceless talent, she was a wonderful musician who could give others pleasure, and no one can take that away.

Thank you, Lord, for music which lifts people at special times.

ER

Singing for God

*The singers were brought together from the region around
Jerusalem... the two choirs that gave thanks
then took their places in the house of God...*

The books of Ezra and Nehemiah give us an almost fly-on-the-wall
insight into the work undertaken by the Jews returning from exile in
Babylon to their holy city. We read there were over 42,000 of them
coming 'home' and bringing with them more than 7,000 servants.
Apart from mentioning camels, mules, horses and donkeys, another
group singled out and recorded for posterity was the group of singers.

These two books catalogue all the free-will offerings made to
finance the reconstruction of the city walls, the opposition they met
and finally the great rededication of the temple. It seems the celebra-
tions were a heady mix of high religious zeal and state pomp with the
ecstatic returned families renewing their allegiance to the God of
Israel. No wonder that the noise of rejoicing could be heard far away.
Indeed, it must have been an awesome occasion when the bulk of the
people lived in little more than caves and tents among the rocks and
olive groves dotted over the hillsides around Jerusalem.

Doesn't it conjure up a wonderful picture! These two choirs,
marching in opposite directions around the completed wall, with
Jezrahiah the conductor, trying to keep them all in order—and in
tune—as they proceeded from the walls into the house of God to take
their official places. What a privilege to be in that choir. Just as spectacular and public an event in its day as for the choir at St Paul's
Cathedral in our time, to be heard all over the world at the Queen's
Golden Jubilee service. Yet both events centred on praising God.

Some of the most sublime music ever written has been inspired by
personal disaster. However, such music, dedicated to the glory of God,
can touch our very soul and bring us peace.

---

*Lord, help me to remember to say 'thank you' more often. Help me to
praise you for all things and not to be embarrassed for other people to
hear and see my joy in the presence of my God.*

Read James 5:13.

ER

Soul music

Speak to one another with psalms, hymns and spiritual songs.
Sing and make music in your heart to the Lord.

In Cornwall there is as great a tradition of singing as in Wales. Like Wales, the number of choirs has declined, but those remaining perform to the highest standards, give enormous pleasure to audiences and raise an amazing amount of money for charity throughout the year. From my 36 years in Cornwall I fondly recall many concert highlights from male voice choirs, ladies' choirs and mixed choirs.

Although mostly accompanied by piano or organ, perhaps some of the most moving songs were when the choir sang unaccompanied. Without the cover of an instrument, the sound was pure 'voice' and one felt the music coming straight from their hearts. There was variety too! Anything from barbershop to *Messiah*, Andrew Lloyd-Webber to Schubert—and all stations in between.

In the middle of one concert, the person chairing the evening suddenly asked the organist to play a line of a well-known hymn... the tenor line only. It was a very well-known hymn but nobody in the audience could guess which hymn. Next the organist played the contralto line on its own and the audience looked truly baffled.

They couldn't make head or tail of the individual 'parts' until, having totally given up, the organist burst forth with 'To God be the glory, great things he has done'. As soon as they heard the first three chords *everyone* knew the hymn.

The point being made was that we are all interdependent upon one another. To create harmony in life we need each one to sing their line; it may sound thin, maybe even boring on its own and hard to get right but, together with the 'air', the Holy Spirit, the music speaks from heart to heart.

Thank you Lord, for the music which has touched my soul. Help me, whether I am 'listening' or taking 'part', to do everything for your praise and glory.

Read 1 Corinthians 12:12–27.

                                                                    ER

Decision-making

He rejected the advice that the older men gave him,
and consulted the young men who had grown up with him and
now attended him. He said to them, 'What do you advise
that we answer this people who have said to me,
"Lighten the yoke that your father put on us"?'

In the last issue of *Day by Day with God*, we read from the early chapters in 2 Chronicles about King Solomon—wise and wealthy, but led into false gods and evil practices by his multitudinous wives and mistresses. God warned him that, as a result, his kingdom would be split. This book focuses on Solomon's descendants—18 kings spanning nearly four centuries—and their rule in Jerusalem over the southern kingdom of Judah.

After 40 years as king, Solomon was succeeded by his son Rehoboam. Soon a deputation arrived. Its leader, Jeroboam, was originally a trusted overseer in Solomon's work force; but Solomon, afraid of being usurped, tried to kill him, and he fled to Egypt until Solomon's death. The deputation pleaded for greater leniency from the new king instead of the harsh treatment Solomon had given them. Rehoboam consulted the old, wise advisers who had served his father.

'Listen to them. Be kind to them, and they will serve you well', was their advice. But Rehoboam wanted to exert his new authority, so he rejected the advice he didn't like. It's easy to do that. We decide what we want to do, then look for someone who will agree with us and will back us up. 'Treat them tough', the younger men advised—and Rehoboam listened. This was the final straw that led to Jeroboam's rebellion and the kingdom's division.

Where do you go for advice? It is good to have friends we can trust with our problems, people who will look to God for wisdom to share with us. Of course, the ultimate responsibility for our decision-making is our own. We must not blame others if things go wrong, though if things go right, I hope we give credit to those who helped.

Lord, please give me wisdom in choosing my advisers.

RG

2 Chronicles 12:1–12 (NRSV)

Whose choice?

*The prophet Shemaiah came to Rehoboam and to the officers of
Judah, who had gathered at Jerusalem because of Shishak, and
said to them, 'Thus says the Lord: "You have abandoned me,
so I have abandoned you to the hand of Shishak."'*

'When the rule of Rehoboam was established and he grew strong, he
abandoned the law of the Lord, he and all Israel with him' (v. 1).
Have you ever heard the accusation that 'Christianity is just for
those who need a crutch' or 'Those who can stand by themselves
don't need God'? Maybe that is how Rehoboam thought. 'Things
are going well; the cities are fortified, the government is under control. I don't need God now.'

How wrong he was! I'm not ashamed to admit when I'm weak,
and that I need to lean on God then. But I need to lean on him just
as much when things are going well, when I think I'm strong. That's
when we often forget him. Rehoboam did—and trouble came. A
powerful Egyptian army led by king Shishak invaded Judah, even
reached Jerusalem. Shemaiah came to Rehoboam with stern words.
'You have abandoned me, so I have abandoned you.' Is that fair?
The people of Judah recognized it was. 'The Lord is in the right' (vv.
5 and 6).

We do not always expect God to be just and right. We expect him
to be kind, forgiving, compassionate, loving. And indeed he is. But
he is also holy, righteous and just. Think of our ultimate destination,
after death. Without his forgiveness, none of us would have a hope
of getting into heaven. But many people say, in effect, 'I'm not going
to let God into my life on earth—but I'll expect him to let me into
heaven when I die.' I think that's cheek! If we don't want him now,
will he want us then? The only 'passport' that lets us into his eternal kingdom is the one that has the face of Jesus superimposed on
our own.

---

*Nothing in my hand I bring,
Simply to thy cross I cling.*
A.M.TOPLADY (1740–78)

RG

Who is on the Lord's side?

Listen to me, Jeroboam and all Israel… Have you not driven out the priests of the Lord, the descendants of Aaron… and made priests for yourselves like the peoples of other lands?… As for us, the Lord is our God, and we have not abandoned him.

Abijah, the new king of Judah, with an army of 400,000, faced Jeroboam, king of Israel, with an army twice that size. Abijah addressed his opponents confidently. 'We are obeying God; he is with us as our leader. But you have abandoned him. You have got golden calves as gods. Israelites, don't fight against the God of your fathers, for you won't succeed.' I like Abijah's confidence. He was not trusting in his own virtue or obedience, or in the faithfulness of his people and their priests. 'The people of Israel prevailed, because they relied on the Lord, the God of their ancestors' (v. 18). They knew he was the God who had brought their people out of Egypt and—miraculously—across the Red Sea; that was the biggest event in their history. He was the God who had established them in the promised land. He was indeed a God on whom they could rely. Stop for a moment, and think of ways in which you have known God in action in your own life, or in the lives of people you know. Is he trustworthy?

Of course, their obedience was important. It enabled them to keep connected with this trustworthy God. God never stops loving us. But if we walk off in the wrong direction, away from him, copying the ways of those who don't bother about Jesus, he is going to seem far away and unreliable—not because he has distanced himself from us but because we have distanced ourselves from him.

Lord, I want to share Abijah's confidence in you. Please show me how reliable you are, and help me to rely on you more.

Trust and obey,
for there's no other way
To be happy in Jesus,
but to trust and obey.
JOHN HENRY SAMMIS (1846–1919)

RG

Spring cleaning

*Asa did what was good and right in the sight of the Lord his God.
He took away the foreign altars and the high places, broke down
the pillars, hewed down the sacred poles, and commanded Judah
to seek the Lord, the God of their ancestors.*

Things aren't always what they seem on the surface! For all Abijah's
protestations about his trust in God and the correctness of the temple worship (13:10, 11), 1 Kings 15:3 tells us that 'he committed all
the sins that his father did before him; his heart was not true to the
Lord his God'. Under the veneer of responsibility and faith was the
substructure of pagan worship. But Asa 'did what was good and right
in the sight of the Lord'. Before he could head a nation that would
be solid in faith he organized the destruction of all the places of
pagan worship throughout the land. Another translation says he
'smashed the sacred stones'. No restraint there in the demolition
process!

Then, after the clearance, he could rebuild. It's like that when we
spring clean in our homes. We can see a job that needs to be tack-
led, but halfway through the process of cleaning and sorting the
mess can seem worse than ever! But, once finished, there is new
peace and order in the home.

What about the spiritual spring cleaning in our own lives? It is
good to stop and take stock sometimes. Are our relationships with
other people as good as they could be? How is our relationship with
God? Does our lifestyle need to change in any way? Are there hidden sins or resentment clogging us? Spring cleaning is usually hard
work, it may even be painful, with prayers of repentance, letters of
apology, prayers to forgive those who have hurt us. But God can
take us through it all, and enable us to rebuild in new peace and
spiritual prosperity.

'Asa did what was good and right in the sight of the Lord his God.'
Wouldn't that be a wonderful epitaph to have on our tombstones!

RG

God with us

'Hear me, Asa and all Judah and Benjamin. The Lord is with you, while you are with him. If you seek him, he will be found by you, but if you abandon him, he will abandon you...
Take courage! Do not let your hands be weak,
for your work shall be rewarded.'

'Do not fear, for I am with you', we read many times in the Bible. That is a wonderful promise. But our verses today remind us of a condition: 'The Lord is with you, while you are with him.' We must not take him for granted, for 'If you abandon him, he will abandon you.' He wants us to be his friends, not just casual acquaintances— and friendships take time to cultivate.

How do we cultivate our friendship with Jesus? It starts in our Bible reading; let him speak to our minds, our wills and our hearts. Then talk to him in prayer about what he has said. As the day goes on, obey him, and talk to him at many odd moments. To my shame, it is only too easy to let a day go by without having remembered that Jesus is with me.

Another thing I notice in today's verses is the encouragement to persevere. Are there struggles in your life at present? Verse 7 reminds me of some words in Hebrews 12: 'Strengthen your weak hands and feeble knees... Fix our eyes on Jesus, who endured the cross... and sat down on the right hand of the throne of God.' Jesus sits now in glory beside his Father, but he has also lived on earth. He has experienced human pressures, difficulties, emotions. He understands our lives from the inside, not just with divine X-ray eyes. And the Spirit who 'came upon' Azariah is the Spirit who has 'permanent residence status' in a Christian, who makes our friendship with Jesus a living reality.

Lord, thank you that you want me as your friend. Help me to listen to you in my Bible reading and my prayer, and to remember you in the busyness of each day.

RG

Courage to confront

King Asa also deposed his grandmother Maacah from her
position as queen mother, because she had made a repulsive
Asherah pole. Asa cut the pole down, broke it up
and burned it in the Kidron Valley.

This may seem a strange choice for our keynote verse today! I have
not chosen it to underline Asa's commitment to clearing the country of the prevalent Baal worship, important though that is, but
because he showed a quality many of us, and many of our leaders,
lack—the courage to confront people who are in the wrong.

In that culture the 'first lady' of the land was not the king's wife,
but his mother. Maacah was the favourite among King Rehoboam's
wives (11:21) and after her son Abijah's short rule ended she kept
her status as queen mother through to her grandson Asa's reign. She
was a woman of power! So it was no small thing for Asa to demol-
ish her statue to the fertility goddess Asherah. It was an even bigger
thing for him to depose her from her position as queen mother.

Confrontation does not have to be aggressive and angry. It can
be gentle as well as firm, whether we are sticking out against injustice or sin that is being done to us personally or to other people.
Jesus told us in Matthew 18:15 (NRSV) how to behave when we
have a personal grievance: 'If another member of your church sins
against you, go and point out the fault when the two of you are
alone.' Take it wider only if they ignore you. It is no mistake that this
paragraph is followed immediately by Peter's question, 'Lord, if
another member of my church sins against me, how often should I
forgive? As many as seven times?' Jesus' answer (whether 77 or 70
times seven) is in effect 'until you've lost count'. An attitude of forgiveness, with a desire for reconciliation and restoration, can enable
confrontation to be firm without anger.

If you have a grievance, pray like this: 'Lord, please show me if, how
and when to speak in this situation.'

RG

Whom do you trust?

Asa took silver and gold from the treasures of the house of the Lord and the king's house, and sent them to king Ben-hadad of Aram, who resided in Damascus, saying 'Let there be an alliance between me and you.'

To understand the story, picture the map: Israel had Judah on its southern border, Aram to its north-east. Asa, king of Judah, felt threatened. Israel had fortified Ramah, the main border town on the route north of Jerusalem, to stop traffic between the two countries. Earlier in his reign Asa had been far more aggressively threatened by the Cushites' vast army. Then his response had been to cry out to God: 'Help us, O Lord, for we rely on you, and in your name we have come against this multitude' (14:11). But now he had, apparently, forgotten the overwhelming victory God gave him. Instead he stole the treasures from the temple and the palace in order to bribe support from Ben-hadad, king of Aram. When Ben-hadad's forces raided Israel's northern cities, Baasha king of Israel diverted his troops from Ramah. The pressure on Asa was relieved—but at what cost! Instead of relying on a faithful, mighty God he depended on bribing a godless king.

Asa's short-term strategy worked, but his folly is plain; we will see its consequences tomorrow. But do we never share his misdirected trust? I think of a big mistake in my own life, in a friendship with another middle-aged woman. We were both long-term Christians, in positions of leadership in our church. We worked together in ministry, we prayed together, we shared our joys and our sorrows; gradually, subtly, we grew too dependent on each other. A friendship that I believe God gave for our mutual support became a snare that took our eyes off him. When she tried to put things right, I refused. The repercussions were huge and destructive. Beware!

Turn your eyes upon Jesus,
look full in his wonderful face;
and the things of earth will grow strangely dim
in the light of his glory and grace.
H.H. LEMMEL

RG

A slippery slope

Then Asa was angry with the seer, and put him in stocks in prison, for he was in a rage with him because of this. And Asa inflicted cruelties on some of the people at the same time.

It is sad to see a fine leader go down the drain ('down the tube' as they say in North America). Maybe the first crack in Asa's whole-heartedness was seen in Friday's reading, in 15:17: 'The high places were not taken out of Israel', although 'the heart of Asa was true all his days'. Yesterday we saw the weakness clearly, when he turned to king Ben-hadad, rather than to God, for support. That was why the prophet Hanani rebuked him in no uncertain terms. There is a warning for us here. Apparently innocuous weeds in the garden of our lives can take hold if they are not rooted out quickly.

When he heard Hanani's words, Asa had a choice. He could have admitted his wrong; humility at this point might have changed the conclusion that 'from now on you will have wars'. Instead he allowed his anger to erupt. First he imprisoned Hanani. Then, having got a taste of blood, he turned on innocent people.

I know only too much about anger in my own life, and am left wondering what was latent in Asa that led to such violence. For myself, I guess that the first seeds of anger were sown when my father died when I was an infant. It remained dormant until I was an adult. Then there was a period when disappointment, or a child's small misdemeanour, would trigger a volcanic response. It became a habit. I was ashamed afterwards, but seemed unable to change. The turning point came when I renounced the chronic attitude that said, 'When I am hurt I have a right to be angry.' Renounce is a strong word that says 'I am determined to change, with God's help.' Since then, God's spring cleaning has transformed me and my relationships.

Thank you, Lord, that with you nothing is impossible.

RG

Remember your lessons

In the thirty-ninth year of his reign Asa was diseased in his feet, and his disease became severe; yet even in his disease he did not seek the Lord, but sought help from the physicians.

Hadn't Asa learnt his lesson? When he relied on God, he was victorious. When he relied on Ben-hadad, trouble came. Now the 'threat' was in a different form—disease in his feet. But again he forgot God, and looked for help from human sources. No doubt he paid for the best doctors, but they could not cure him.

I have good reason to remember this verse. After a week in hospital after an operation, I went home to convalesce, but my recuperation was slower than expected. One Sunday I 'happened' to be reading this chapter. This verse leapt out at me, almost as if God himself had used a highlighting pen. Wow! I had been relying on the doctors, not looking as well to God for his healing touch. I not only prayed myself, but asked others in my church to pray for me (and the way that happened clearly had God's hand on it). My recovery immediately speeded up.

Fifteen years later I was preparing a talk on king Asa, and planned to refer to this incident in my own life. A niggling infection hampered my concentration, but I struggled on. That evening I dragged myself, reluctantly, to a meeting with a small group of friends. 'May we pray for you with this infection?' Debbie asked. Wow! Here was I planning to criticize Asa and relate my own experience of healing in answer to prayer—and yet again I had forgotten to ask God for his help and his healing. How often we forget the lessons that we believe we have learnt from God.

Can you look back at your own life and see ways in which God has needed to show you the same truth time and time again? Ask him to help you to learn, to remember and to put into practice the things he teaches you.

RG

Teach the word

*In his early years [Jehoshaphat] walked in the ways his father
David had followed... In the third year of his reign he sent his
officials... to teach in the towns of Judah... They taught
throughout Judah, taking with them the Book of the
Law of the Lord.*

'In his early years...' When I first read that phrase I thought the
writer was talking about the years of Jehoshaphat's youth. Then I
realized that he is referring to the early years of Jehoshaphat's reign.
But those two are not disconnected. The standards and behaviour
of a 30-year-old are most often set in the foundation of childhood.
Proverbs 22:6 makes that clear: 'Train children in the right way, and
when old they will not stray' (NRSV). And Jehoshaphat did not
only want to obey God himself; he wanted his people to do the
same. So early on in his reign he sent out some of his officials to go
throughout the land teaching from the scriptures. I hope the people
were enthused. I'm not sure which I think is a greater crime in
Christian leaders: to fail to teach the Bible at all, or to teach in such
a way that people switch off in boredom.

Jehoshaphat reminds me of Timothy nine centuries later.
Timothy was brought up by his godly mother and grandmother, who
taught him well from the Old Testament scriptures. And Paul was
concerned that Timothy should not only stay faithful himself, but
that he should pass on the truth to others who would themselves
become teachers (2 Timothy 1:5; 3:14, 15; 2:2).

In what ways can you not only learn God's truth for yourself but
also pass it on to others—in your family, in your church, in your
place of work, with your friends? When our own children were
young we had great fun with bedtime Bible stories; now I am glad to
see them doing the same with their own children. It is a great privilege to teach others the word by which we ourselves seek to live.

Please help me to share your truth.

RG

Learn to listen

Micaiah said, 'As the Lord lives, whatever my God says, that will I speak'… [Zedekiah asked] 'Which way did the spirit of the Lord pass from me to you?' Micaiah replied, 'You will find out on that day when you go to hide in an inner chamber.'

Today's reading is a long one, but to make sense of the situation we cannot easily prune it. At first sight it seems a strange story—yet the people in it have a familiar ring. Do you know anyone who fits the characters of Ahab, Jehoshaphat, Zedekiah or Micaiah? Ahab, king of Israel, wanted to hear only smooth words from the prophets. Jehoshaphat, king of Israel, really wanted to know what God wanted. Zedekiah was the leader of 400 so-called prophets, who stuck together in their words, giving reassurance to the king. Micaiah, the man of God, was determined to hear and to speak God's truth. He did not change his tune even when he was slapped into prison on a diet of bread and water.

I want to focus on Micaiah. Read verses 12 and 13 again. Already aware of the king's antagonism towards him (v. 7), was it hard for him to resist the messenger's pressure (v. 12)? It is a temptation that comes to many of us. 'Go with the crowd. Don't worry about your scruples. Play safe. Conform.' Micaiah was set on being true to God. I don't think he even wobbled, despite his initial favourable reply to King Ahab in verse 14. Then he came out with the true story: disaster for the Israelites, lies from the mouths of the prophets. No wonder Zedekiah was angry when his deceit was unmasked!

Micaiah's answer shows us the secret of his ability to listen to God: 'Go to hide in an inner room…' That is a word for us in our busy world. The greater the pressures and demands in our lives, the more important it is to find the space to get alone with God, to read, think, pray, listen—to discover what he wants to say to us.

Lord, help me to really listen to you today.

RG

2 Chronicles 19:1–10 (NIV)

Dispensing justice

Consider carefully what you do, because you are not judging for man but for the Lord, who is with you whenever you give a verdict. Now let the fear of the Lord be upon you. Judge carefully, for with the Lord our God there is no injustice or partiality or bribery.

'Mummy, it's not fair. Jane's got more than me...', 'It wasn't my fault, Miss. Johnny threw it first...'. Jehoshaphat was giving this charge to the men he had appointed as judges in the cities of Judah. But he gives good principles for any of us who, in a position of authority, may be called to settle disputes or to mete out punishment. Home, school, work, the sports field... you may have responsibilities in other spheres, too.

- 'Consider carefully': We often act impulsively under the pressure of the moment; but we can weigh a response with care, even if it has to be speedy.
- 'You are not judging for people, but for the Lord': The framework for our verdict is not just the people we can see in front of us, but the invisible God who is the judge.
- 'He is with you, whenever you give a verdict': I am reminded of James, who wrote, 'If any of you lacks wisdom, ask God... and it will be given him' (James 1:5). This asking does not have to be an extensive prayer; even in the heat of the moment we can say a quick, 'Lord, please show me your way now.'
- 'Let the fear of the Lord be upon you': This is not the fear of being afraid, but the fear that stands in awe of God.
- 'With the Lord our God there is no injustice or partiality or bribery': That is the sort of judge our God is. May we reflect him whenever we are called on to give out a verdict.

A prayer based on verse 11: 'Lord, I pray that I may act with courage at all times, specially when I am called on to settle a dispute or to mete out punishment.'

RG

Helpless!

Messengers came and told Jehoshaphat, 'A great multitude is coming against you from Edom.'... Jehoshaphat stood in the assembly of Judah... 'We are powerless against this great multitude that is coming against us. We do not know what to do, but our eyes are on you.'

Jehoshaphat was in trouble. A huge army was only 20 miles from Jerusalem. What was he to do? In a similar situation many of us would panic, or call a committee meeting. Jehoshaphat didn't. He set himself to seek God, and called the people to fast and pray with him. Notice the pattern of his prayer in verses 6 to 12: a) God and his power, b) God's past actions, c) the expectancy that God would answer prayer, d) the immediate need, e) the plea of faith. That is a good pattern for us to use for our own intercession; too often we plunge in, and tell God what we think he ought to do for us. Jehoshaphat's attitude—like that of his father Asa in his early days (14:11)—was, 'We can't, but you can.' And indeed God did act in a remarkable way next day, as we read in verses 22 to 24. The victory was not won by Jehoshaphat's troops, but by the enemy soldiers killing one another!

God does not always act in such a spectacular way, nor so speedily. But he is faithful, and he is a God who makes no mistakes—no, none, although we cannot always see it. This morning I have spent time with two people who are both running right up to the eleventh hour (one might even say, 11.59) on finding a job. I read these verses to each of them. They saw the point! When you feel totally overwhelmed, don't ignore the problem, but focus on God, not on the difficulties.

O Lord, are you not the God who is in heaven? Power and might are in your hand. So I come to talk about (any difficulty you have at present). I do not know what to do, but my eyes are upon you.

RG

Trust and obey

*They rose early in the morning and went out into the
wilderness of Tekoa; and as they went out, Jehoshaphat stood
and said, 'Listen to me, O Judah and inhabitants of Jerusalem!
Believe in the Lord your God and you will be established;
believe his prophets.'*

The threat from the enemy forces had not changed—except that
they were even nearer Jerusalem—but Jehoshaphat had. Yesterday
we read of his fear and helplessness when he heard about the
approaching enemy. In weakness he prayed to a trustworthy God.

God's first answer to that prayer came through Jahaziel. His message was clear and confident. Read verses 15 to 17 again (aloud if
possible): 'Do not fear or be dismayed because of this vast army.' Is
there an 'enemy' in your life of which you are afraid—a person, a situation, something difficult you have to do? Sometimes even a triv-
ial act can seem huge… a phone call to make, a letter to write, a
decision about money. 'Do not be afraid; do not be dismayed. Go
out to face them tomorrow' (it may even be today!), 'and the Lord
will be with you.' Time and time again we read in the Bible, 'Do not
be afraid, for I am with you'. I love that. God knows how often we
are afraid; we need to be reminded frequently that fear can be over-
come by the assurance of his presence, like a frightened child
clutching an adult's hand.

They did not waste time in obeying. 'Early in the morning' they
set out. I once learnt a painful lesson about the folly of procrastina-
tion. In the spring God made it clear: 'Put that situation right.' 'Yes,
Lord, I will—when the summer holidays are over and church life
starts up again.' But before I acted, the situation crashed. My obedience was theoretical, the delay costly. When God says, 'Do it', he
wants obedience now, not later.

---

*Lord, my current 'enemy' is………… Please show me how to act.
Take my fear. Encourage me with your presence. Help me to obey.*
                                                                    RG

Ann Warren's husband, Peter, died a few months after the following notes were written. Ann shares with us how their belief and trust in God's promises and the love and prayers of Christian friends helped them both as they walked through the valley. These notes will help us all to understand the importance of the words of St Paul, 'to live is Christ and to die is gain' (Philippians 1:21, NIV).

The valley of the shadow

The Lord is my shepherd, I shall not be in want. He makes me lie down in green pastures, he leads me beside quiet waters, he restores my soul... Even though I walk through the valley of the shadow of death, I will fear no evil, for you are with me; your rod and your staff, they comfort me.

Eighteen months ago we received the dreaded news that my husband had cancer. I can still remember the exact moment in the consultant's waiting room and the stunning, almost physical blow with which these frightening words hit us. Worse still, since numerous previous visits to the doctor had failed to correctly diagnose this problem, his disease had already become secondary and effectively terminal.

It seemed that the valley of the shadow of death lay straight ahead of us along a deep, dark road with no possible way of escape. At that moment God and all his promises seemed a million miles away, and we found ourselves crying out to the seemingly empty heavens, 'How could you allow this to happen?'

But however terrible the future seemed, we knew in our hearts that he would not leave us without the comfort of his presence. Somewhere, beyond the fear and the hopelessness, we knew we had a saviour and friend who had been through the very dregs of human suffering himself—and who had promised to be alongside us all even in the depths of our despair.

For all of us this is the bottom line of our faith. How will we cope when some terrible accident, the loss of a loved one, devastating financial loss or sudden unemployment remove our earthly security in one shattering blow?

Dear Lord, we know that you are the good shepherd and that you have promised to lead us beside quiet waters and to restore our souls. As we pass through the valley of the shadow, keep us safe from the fear of evil and help us to really trust you with the future, whatever lies ahead.

AW

One day at a time

'So do not worry, saying, "What shall we eat?" or "What shall we drink?" or "What shall we wear?" For the pagans run after all these things, and your heavenly father knows that you need them. But seek first his kingdom and his righteousness, and all these things will be given you as well. Therefore do not worry about tomorrow, for tomorrow will worry about itself. Each day has enough trouble of its own.'

The only way to travel through the valley of the shadow is to learn to live one day at a time, without worrying about what the future holds. Needless to say, that is incredibly difficult to do! Always lurking over the horizon is the next fearful diagnosis, someone else who is very ill, or the memory of other painful bereavements.

Having lost both my parents by the age of seven I found it almost impossible at first not to cross this bridge well ahead of time. But worrying about what lay ahead meant that we both became completely eaten up by this and consequently lost sight of all joy and happiness in our present lives.

Many of the things we waste hours of emotional energy worrying about in life never actually happen, and in the meantime we can be unnecessarily taken over and preoccupied by these fears. Our heavenly Father has promised to give us the help and strength to cope *when we need it and not before*. It is impossible for us to calculate beforehand what our needs or our reactions will be—he alone knows and is waiting lovingly in the wings to help us when the time comes.

Take time to look back over your life and recollect how God has helped you through a crisis in the past. Lift to him any problems or worries that you have, praying for a real sense of his peace and an ability to trust him with whatever the future holds.

Heavenly Father, help me never to allow the joy of today to be snatched away by the fear of tomorrow.

AW

God's window

No temptation has seized you except what is common to man.
And God is faithful; he will not let you be tempted beyond what
you can bear. But when you are tempted, he will also provide a
way out so that you can stand up under it.

This is one of the very first Bible verses I learnt—and it has so often
come to my rescue whenever trouble has struck.

Sometimes the verse has been paraphrased another way: 'If God
shuts a door he always opens a window.' However impossible it may
seem when life looks really black, God's window will always open
out over the most unexpected viewpoint which can really lift your
spirits. And we have personally experienced this even in the valley
of the shadow.

As soon as the news of Peter's illness got around, we were
absolutely overwhelmed by the love and support of friends, both
from our local church and much further afield. It was astonishing
how many people came out of the woodwork—cards, letters, messages of help, which—while they could not take away the pain—
somehow surrounded us with a glow of love like a warm cocoon.
Strengthened by this love it has felt at times almost as if Jesus himself was travelling the same road alongside us—just as he had
promised.

Peter was completely bowled over by the affirmations and things
people said to him. With our normal British stiff upper lip much of
this would usually have been kept for the funeral! He particularly
appreciated those who did not know what to say but who tried anyway. It was all such an overwhelming expression of love and support
that we were left wondering why it takes this sort of experience to
bring us to affirm and encourage friends who are precious to us?

Ask God to help you to reach out and affirm friends and colleagues—
even the difficult ones—and for the ability to 'love one another as he
has loved us'.

AW

Where are you heading?

'Do not let your hearts be troubled. Trust in God; trust also in me. In my Father's house are many rooms; if it were not so, I would have told you. I am going there to prepare a place for you. And if I go and prepare a place for you, I will come back and take you to be with me that you also may be where I am.'

We are all going to die, but this is a highly unpopular subject in the 21st century! Death today is usually hidden safely away from view behind closed hospital doors, but in past centuries the death-bed scene was familiar to everyone as a normal part of life. Now only major tragedies such as the destruction of the World Trade Centre in New York with the death of some 3,000 people force this briefly into our conscious minds.

Living in the valley of the shadow completely alters the perspective of life, because our eyes are suddenly focused on a different destination. When we realize that we are actually on our way to heaven to spend eternity in the presence of Jesus, our priorities become very different.

Suddenly we discover, perhaps for the very first time in our lives, what is really important—the love and warmth of family and friends, watching the children grow, the beauty of nature all around us. For each one of us it will be different, but one thing we do know—it will not be those things that most people chase after. No man ever said on his death-bed, 'I wish I had spent more time at the office!'

Take time to think about your life now and how much time and energy you are investing in eternity. What could you change in order to get ready for your heavenly destination?

Dear Lord, when I am overtaken by the material concerns of life, please help me never to forget where I am going and what this life is really about.

AW

Fruit that will last

'My command is this: Love each other as I have loved you.
Greater love has no one than this, that he lay down his life
for his friends. You are my friends if you do what I command.
I no longer call you servants because a servant does not
know his master's business. Instead, I have called you friends
for everything that I learned from my Father I have made
known to you. You did not choose me but I chose you
to go and bear fruit—fruit that will last.'

One thing that has always struck me about people who have just survived some terrible trauma or tragedy is that they return to their everyday lives with a whole new perspective, and a determination to make each day count for something. Above all they try to really show love to people around them. They have finally realized that the life they so nearly lost is really precious and never to be wasted again.

I wonder what difference it would make to your life today if you knew that this was your last week on earth? Perhaps you might regret terribly not having forgiven someone who has wronged you? I wonder if your friends and family really know how much you love them? What would you want to leave behind you when you go?

Take time to try and identify 'fruit that will last' in your life. Try writing an honest obituary about yourself and look for the gaps and things you would like to change in as many years as you have left. These may not be very 'big' things, and they probably will not seem very important now, but remember that in the eyes of our Lord the commands about loving one another come top of the list.

Dear heavenly Father, please lay on my heart today those things that
you would have me do before it is too late—those I need to forgive or
help or simply telephone to let them know I care about them.

AW

A glimpse of eternity

*He has made everything beautiful in its time. He has also set
eternity in the hearts of men; yet they cannot fathom what God
has done from beginning to end. I know that there is nothing
better for men than to be happy and to do good while they live.
That every man may eat and drink, and find satisfaction in all his
toil—this is the gift of God.*

Many people have had some tiny glimpse of eternity during their
lifetime on earth. A moment of transcendent joy at the sight of a
magnificent red-gold sunset filling the western sky; the wonder of
seeing a tiny helpless child for the first time; the sight of thousands
of spring leaves and flowers filling the barren gardens after the win-
ter; and even moments when it seems that God himself has reached
down to earth in the middle of a church service or at the communion rail—then all too often it is gone in a flash.

But we all have this deep longing for eternity in our hearts—and
despite today's culture that tells us that we can stay young and keep
on going, we know perfectly well we are not immortal. The ancient
Egyptians did their best to prepare for eternity by mummifying their
pharaohs and providing all that they might need for the after-life,
but we know a better, more certain, way.

'Now this is eternal life: that they may know you, the only true
God, and Jesus Christ, whom you have sent' (John 17:3). Eternal life
is about knowing who we believe in and about travelling on through
life beside him until we go to be with him.

Sometimes this experience is so real for Christians that they can
actually sense Jesus there beside them as they come close to death.
'Can't you see him?' people have been heard to say, 'He was here just
a moment ago.'

---

*Dear Lord Jesus, please hold on to me as I travel through the problems
of life, and help me to know without any doubts that you will be there
for me when the time for eternity comes, however long it takes.*

AW

Death comes to us all

For I know that through your prayers and the help given by the Spirit of Jesus Christ, what has happened to me will turn out for my deliverance. I eagerly expect and hope that I will in no way be ashamed, but will have sufficient courage so that now as always Christ will be exalted in my body, whether by life or by death. For me to live is Christ and to die is gain.

For many years these verses have really challenged me about life, and now they have an even greater poignancy about what lies ahead of us. For Peter the question is of course 'Am I ready to let go of everything on this earth that is so precious, and even more to the point, am I ready to meet my Maker face to face?' As for myself, can I honestly say that to live on alone is 'gain'?

Nothing concentrates the mind more effectively on what is really important in life than the imminent possibility of death—it has the same effect as holding up a compass to check where our lives are heading. And more importantly it also gives us the opportunity to change course before it is too late.

Most young people try not to think about this subject at all, with the supreme confidence that it will probably be many years before they ever need to face up to this painful issue. But as we have seen recently with the sudden deaths of the thousands of young professional people who went innocently off to work one fine morning in New York, there are no guarantees in this life.

It is said that William Grimshaw, one of the leading figures in the 18th-century revival, had vowed from a very early age to think of his own death every single day of his life—and that as a result he was 'mightily used'.

Heavenly Father, please give me the courage to face up to my own mortality and through this to see where my life is leading.

AW

Holiness

Be holy because I, the Lord your God, am holy. Each of you must respect his mother and father, and you must observe my Sabbaths.

God's burning desire for his people to be like him in holiness rings out from the Bible again and again. But what does it mean? We may sing about it often in church but do we ever ask, what is God's holiness, exactly?

Is it, as the verse above implies, about behaviour or moral goodness—respecting our parents, the sabbath and so on? Apart from the small difficulty that, as God doesn't have parents it's hard to imitate him in that respect, how can we possibly be as good as he is? Is it about not contaminating ourselves? Leviticus 11:44 says, 'Consecrate yourselves and be holy, because I am holy. Do not make yourselves unclean by any creature that moves about on the ground.' Could ritual cleansing and eating the right food make us holy? Women's magazines suggest that to be acceptable to other people, we need to pay attention to cleansing and diet regimes but, these days, most Christians aren't too worried about these things in relation to God.

Is holiness about divine qualities, the awesome 'God-ness' of God? Revelation 15:3 says, 'You alone are holy.' In which case how *can* human beings be holy? You can see that I have lots of questions—and probably lots of misconceptions. To be honest I feel a bit negative about holiness, it's offputting, perhaps dangerous—an impossible standard which makes me feel guilty. It's also a huge subject on which learned theologians have written tomes, so I'm probably stepping into a mine-field but I wondered if it was something we might look at and pray through together?

Dear Lord, sometimes I know I'm in your holy presence and I don't have too many questions then, all I can do is to worship you. But I need your illumination on this wonder if I'm to even begin to enter into your heart's desire for me to be holy, as you are holy.

CL

Touching holiness

The men of Beth Shemesh asked, 'Who can stand in the presence of the Lord, this holy God? To whom will the ark go up from here?'

The visible sign of God's holiness was the precious ark of the covenant. Captured by Israel's enemies, the Philistines, it brought such grief that they begged to return it, sending gold in expiation, setting it loose on a cart drawn by two cows separated from their calves. A sign-miracle headed it towards Israel's border-village of Beth Shemesh.

People there worshipped God rejoicing but, 'God struck down some of the men of Beth Shemesh, putting seventy of them to death because they had looked into the ark of the Lord.' Hardly surprising that the rest wanted rid of it. Years later, after the unfortunate Uzzah tried to steady it against falling and was struck dead, even good King David was so afraid to take it to Jerusalem he left it with a *foreigner*, a Gittite called Obed-Edom. If holiness is more dangerous and unpredictable than powerful magic, annihilating people without allowing for spontaneous curiosity or protective instincts—who needs it?

And us? Are we scared that this holy God will destroy us? His awesome holiness encompasses all of his other attributes. The Bible tells us, often, to fear him. He's certainly not some kind of 'mate' on our own level. But then, if he acted regularly with the kind of capricious dangerousness which these strange old stories suggest, who would be left in this world? I believe his holiness means, as C.S. Lewis said of his Christ-lion Aslan, that while God's not tame, he is good!

Holy God, we don't want to enclose you in a box: that was always dangerous. Nor to make you in our image. You are other than us. Yes, we're in awe of you—but have experienced too much of your love and grace to run away now. We can only worship you, in Spirit and in truth—giving thanks that you, the most holy God, can and do live among us.

CL

Holy wholeness

The ark of the Lord remained in the house of Obed-Edom the Gittite for three months, and the Lord blessed him and his entire household.

'Separate', 'set aside'—that is what the word translated 'holy' means, in both New Testament Greek and Old Testament Hebrew. So is a holy God like some alien matter—if human beings touch him, we die? Although we could read that into the stories mentioned in yesterday's reading, most of scripture doesn't bear it out, nor does our experience. How many people have you seen struck dead by God as Uzzah was? I've known occasions when people weren't able to stand in the presence of God, rather like the priests who were there when his glory fell on the tabernacle and 'couldn't stand to minister'. Afterwards, though, they seemed more alive— alive to God, alive to his love, his peace and, often, to a new vision for what he wanted to do with their lives. The English word 'holy' comes from the Saxon for 'whole' or 'sound'. Yes, encounters with the holiness of God make people more whole and sound, though sometimes they remain broken… if that makes sense.

The strange story of the dangerous ark turns. It 'remained in the house of Obed-Edom the Gittite for three months and the Lord blessed him and his entire household' before David carried it back to Jerusalem 'with rejoicing'. And Obed-Edom? Though a foreigner, he turns up again in Chronicles as a harpist, leading worship in the temple, ministering regularly before the ark like the best of Levites. He also became a temple gatekeeper, looking after its holy treasures as did 62 of his descendants, for generations.

One of the Bible's forgotten heroes, Obed-Edom's world appears to have been transformed after the holy presence of God resided for three months in his house. His name appears in 1 Chronicles 13, 15, 16, 25–26. You might like to look him up and have a think about what his story means for you.

CL

Wholly at the centre

If you return to the Almighty, you will be restored: If you remove
wickedness from your tent and assign... your gold of Ophir to the
rocks in the ravines, then the Almighty will be your gold... surely
then you will find delight in [him].

When I asked what holiness meant to people in our home-group,
the youngest woman replied, 'Well, you know—that passage in Job
about the gold of Ophir!'

'No!' the rest of us chorused. 'What passage in Job?' I know the
beginning and end of that book but have ignored the pages of
unhelpful advice given by the unfortunate man's 'friends'. Here
though is a little nugget. It concerns the question of what is the
most precious thing in our lives? If God is at the very centre, we
remain whole and holy. Nothing can separate him from us. Should
everything else be stripped away, we'll have all we need because, like
Job, we'll be able to say, 'I know that my Redeemer lives... and after
my skin has been destroyed, yet in my flesh I will see God' (Job
19:25–26). By delighting in him we'll become holy quite naturally,
because we'll do only what pleases him.

Sometimes we turn away from him to make other things the centre of our lives. If those things are 'wickedness' we need to chuck
them out. Often they are perfectly good things which have become
overly precious to us, such as the 'gold' of particular people who are
dear to us, of our homes, churches, or even of prayer itself. Of course
we don't have to throw these things into a ravine but we won't find
holiness, or true happiness, unless God and his agenda are once
more at the centre of our lives and relationships, until we rest our
security purely in his love, which came first and will last for ever.

You say, 'I am rich; I have acquired wealth and do not need a thing...'
I counsel you to buy from me gold refined in the fire.
REVELATION 3:17–18

CL

Holy ordinariness?

Make every effort to live in peace with all men and to be holy:
without holiness no one will see the Lord.

Another person told a true story about holiness, which he'd read in
a book by Rick Joyner. Rick and a friend were queueing at an airport
check-in desk. As take-off time approached, it became clear that
not everyone would get on the plane. Staff weren't the most effi-
cient and complaints of stressed-out passengers only made matters
worse. Then, just as Rick and his friend were reaching the head of
the queue, two large women, complete with trolley-loads of luggage,
attempted to push their way in front of them.

As the queue's aggression reached boiling point, Rick's friend
said to the women, 'Please, take my place and I will go to the back.'
I guess he wasn't simply being polite but trusting God to get him to
wherever he needed to be. The pushy women found themselves in
an invidious position, tension deflated, the atmosphere became co-
operative, check-in staff worked wonders and everyone, including
Rick and his friend, caught the plane.

Rick said that 'ordinary' incident was one of the clearest examples he's experienced of a miracle—an everyday miracle of holy, self-
less love at work. Maybe we can't be holy as God is holy. But if we,
trusting God, behave a little bit more like Jesus would behave,
maybe, like a smile in a gloomy situation, it'll be 'catching'. His holy
rule or kingdom will edge closer. And maybe those with eyes to see
will understand a little bit more about what he is like.

---

*The scary thing is, Lord, I think I'd have pushed back, insisted on my
rights, even felt proud of queueing in a civilized, 'British' way. Your
holy ways don't always feel natural or comfortable to me, even though
I've claimed to follow you for some years. Yet I can see that sin and
selfishness isn't good for people, while your way is! Help me to see—
and then go—your holy way, rather than my own selfish one.*

CL

Holy smoke!

*You also, like living stones, are being built into a spiritual house
to be a holy priesthood, offering spiritual sacrifices acceptable to
God through Christ Jesus… You are a chosen people, a royal
priesthood, a holy nation, a people belonging to God,
that you may declare the praises of him who called you
out of darkness into his wonderful light.*

I've kept asking other Christians what they make of this idea of holiness. One person said, 'I think the most amazing thing is that, within the context of his holiness, God loves *me*! Just think about that!' Grasping that has to be key, doesn't it?

Someone added, 'When Christians are seen as obsessed with sin it's a real barrier to sharing the good news of God's salvation.' But psychologists tell us that the root of much mental illness lies in guilt—guilt or shame. As Christians, we are cleansed and forgiven and lifted up. That's so powerful. The guilt really has gone—and with it our nothingness, our devalued state. We really are being transformed by his power into this amazing 'royal priesthood' and 'holy nation'.

Another quoted, 'Lord I thank you that so far today I've not been irritable, stubborn or selfish. But in a moment I'll have to get out of bed—and that's when I'll really need your help!' Saintly isolation is not what it's all about—but when Christians who have Jesus at the centre of their lives come together, each of us reflects different aspects of his holiness. As the 'house' is more than the stones, the whole is more than the parts. Each of us becomes like the transparent prisms in some glittering chandelier which blazes the light of Jesus abroad. It's not always like that of course—sometimes we get a bit grimy and block the light from one another—but I've known times when it has been. And I guess heaven will be like that chandelier effect only more so. Wonderful!

What does holiness—both individual and corporate—mean to you?

CL

God's holiness affecting our behaviour

Be still before the Lord, all mankind, because he has roused himself from his holy dwelling.

I asked if anyone had a first-hand experience of God's holiness. One replied, 'Yes. I've felt God's holy presence so strongly that I couldn't keep standing. I fell to my knees in awe. That was the immediate effect. And then there was an awakening to what life is all about. His holiness filled my thoughts and prayers, made them alive in a new way.'

Did that make a difference, longer-term? 'I understand now that God is in control. That puts less onus on me. For example at work, he's behind and in front of me. He's so magnificent and different that I can't comprehend him, yet I know I'm in his hands and he's in control. That changes the way I behave.'

Isn't it great that God doesn't stay in some remote 'holy dwelling'—he comes among us, bringing his holiness to make a difference to our lives, sometimes dramatically, as this person described. (Read Isaiah chapter 6 onwards to see how experiencing God's awesome holiness changed the prophet's life.)

Personally I'm relieved that, God being with us, we don't have to work out 'being holy as he is holy' on our own! All Christians start off as 'holy and beloved' (Romans 1:7) and, as we open ourselves to the Holy Spirit, he lives within us through ordinary moments, making us more holy by the day. We can't expect mystical experiences all the time but the Holy Spirit loves us to give him the freedom of every 'room' in the 'house' of our lives, to be still, give him space and watch him at work in us. He doesn't have a compulsive cleaning disorder either—he's not forever seeking dark corners, to evict cobwebs and dry rot. He enjoys our company—simply being at home with us!

Help me be still before you now, Lord—to enjoy your holy presence filling every little compartment and room of my life with warmth and love.

CL

A sinner holy?

The Pharisee stood up and prayed about himself, 'God, I thank you that I am not like other men—robbers, evildoers, adulterers... I fast twice a week and give a tenth of all I get.' ... But the tax collector ... said, 'God, have mercy on me, a sinner.'

Religious show has perhaps put more people off a relationship with God than anything else. 'Holier than thou' is deeply unattractive. 'I'm a Christian and I'm OK; you're not!' far from winning others, separates them from God. Jesus reserved his harshest words for those who thought they were holy and pleasing to God. Isn't it interesting that the Pharisee 'prayed about himself'? Those words imply that he kept God's law, remaining pure and unpolluted, in order to gain 'gold stars' for himself. Having become so self-righteous that he's not even asking God for help, he's lost all concern for others. Most Pharisees felt totally affronted that a rabbi like Jesus would mix with robbers, evildoers, adulterers and cheats.

And me? Well, actually I don't like being with people who smoke, get drunk or swear, who are rude, who tell lies or sleep around. If people are listening to certain radio stations or talking about certain TV programmes which range from distasteful to plain evil I'd rather not spend time with them, thank you. Does this mean I'm truly holy—or pharisaically more concerned about myself than in reaching out to them in love? Am I wise or lacking faith in God who loves and redeems sinners like me... *and* like them? If, relying on the Holy Spirit within me, I reach outside of nice, safe, 'Christian' areas, will I get polluted, catch the sinner's disease—or will the love, grace and righteousness of God mediated even through me 'contaminate' the cancer of evil with the healthy growing cells of goodness?

Teach me your holy path, dear Lord. Help me not to stray from it— to the 'right' of complacent, off-putting 'goodness' or to the 'left' of falling into sin.

CL

Holiness versus evil

Your eyes are too pure to look on evil;
you cannot tolerate wrong.

Does God's holiness make him delicate? Is he like some maiden aunt who can be shocked into a faint? Is evil some super-kryptonite which defeats God by dissolving his fatally vulnerable holy nature? Clearly not, when the whole message of Habakkuk is that, though evil people appear to triumph, God has everything under control and that we can trust him, whatever. Habakkuk asks some searching questions of God and by the end of his prophecies (3:19) he has some amazing answers. God is not weak—instead 'the Sovereign Lord is my strength, he makes my feet like the feet of a deer, he enables me to go on the heights'.

Time and time again God has looked on the wickedness in the world and chosen not to destroy it, 'tolerating wrong' in order to give people yet another chance to respond to his love, grace and goodness. Time and time again Jesus looked evil straight in the eye, and without repaying it with evil, gained the moral (and actual) victory. In the moment when evil did its worst against the holiness of God, salvation was born. We are not dualists, caught up in some equal battle of light and dark, day and night. Self-sacrificing goodness may appear weak and unattractive, evil seductive and powerful. But there's a banality in evil and, as it becomes increasingly ugly and self-defeating, God's holiness and righteousness shine out. They will triumph. We are on the winning side!

What about us? Suppose some kids who attended the holiday Bible club at our church turn up the following Sunday. Not used to sitting still through a service, they disturb the holy and reverent atmosphere. OK, they are not evil but are we shocked into making them feel unwelcome, even asking them to leave? What about the young girl in the youth group who falls pregnant, the church leaders whose marriage breaks up, the children's worker who is caught out telling lies?

CL

Holy violence

Darkness came over the whole land until three in the afternoon...
and the curtain of the temple was torn in two.

As Jesus is crucified like a shameful criminal, at the hands of the
hated Roman army which occupies the promised land, the light
which he brought into the world, along with the sun itself, is extin-
guished. And yet... all is not as it seems. Light dawns for the super-
vising Roman centurion and he proclaims Jesus' innocence.

Jesus' 'strange' brand of holiness, seen as blasphemous by the
spiritual leaders of God's people, provoked them to rig his trial and
arrange his death. God's Son dies! The temple curtain is torn in
two, and the holy of holies, which only the high priest dared enter
once a year, appears to be desecrated—unsurprising, since the evil
within humankind has killed the source, the Creator of life itself.
But... all is not as it seems. We know that Jesus' death made a way
for all who believe in him to reach the holiest place of all. The
power of the temple, which denied women, disabled people and for-
eigners access to any but its outer courts, was broken by God's most
urgent longing for relationship with all of these people.

If Jesus was prepared to endure unthinkable violence in order to
blast a way through the 'curtain' which separated people from God,
if he was prepared to enter the darkest place in order to ensure the
light burned brightly, then who are we to say that we can't approach
his holy presence, can't live in his light? Who are we to say that anyone can't—anyone who faces away from the darkness and turns
towards him?

Lord, sometimes I 'defend' you from my own or other people's puny
attempts to be unholy, as if you needed defending or hiding away, as
if you hadn't proved yourself beyond corruption. Evil is terrible, sin is
destructive—but let me grasp the far greater power of your righteous-
ness to drive away the darkness and resurrect the way from earth to
heaven.

                                                                    CL

Holy exclusion zone?

Be holy as I am holy.

My daughter's eighth birthday fell a few days after her year-group went up from First to Middle School. The big question became—who to ask to the party? Her closest friends of course, but her wider circle was distributed around three different classes in the new school and, in developing new friendships, she would most likely lose touch with many. Of course she wanted *everyone* to her party but large numbers wouldn't have been safe, so we had to make some hard decisions.

A few days later the mother of—we'll call her 'Emily'—phoned in some distress. Had we failed to invite Emily because we thought her 'weird'? Horrified I explained our rationale and tried to tell her that I thought Emily a sweet, little girl. No way would she and 'weird' exist in the same sentence—so where had that idea come from? Had the children been saying things? No, this woman was under the impression that I, and my daughter, thought she, and her daughter, 'weird' because they weren't Christians.

No, how awful! Plenty of people in the school thought *we* were weird, I'm sure, because we were Christians. I knew what it felt like to be excluded, thought odd—and would never want to do this to anyone else. I don't know to this day how it happened, since I genuinely liked Emily and her mother and had spent time chatting happily with both. All I can hope is that I've never given anyone else the impression, before or since, that I think anyone 'weird' or would exclude them because they aren't Christians.

We're good at drawing circles, saying, 'we're inside, you're outside'... of the church, of relationship with God... whatever! But Jesus is calling from the centre, the cross. All that really matters is whether people are turning towards him, or turning away.

You show your holiness, Lord, by inviting everyone. Only those who exclude themselves feel unwelcome. Help me to have the same mind, and to give the same impression, always.

CL

Holiness without walls

'Jerusalem will be a city without walls because of the great
number of men and livestock in it. And I myself will be a wall of
fire around it,' declares the Lord, 'and I will be its glory within.'

It was a television series about Jesus which helped me understand
the monolithic nature of the temple and just what Jesus was fighting against when he overturned the money-changers' tables there—
the power-base he was fighting all his ministry. Modern computer
wizardry reconstructed the Jerusalem of his day—and the towering
walls of the temple made people look like ants. The USSR's Kremlin
and Bejing's Forbidden City had nothing on those walls, which were
there to exclude people, progressively, in categories—women, non-
Jews, those whose bodies were disabled or imperfect in any way,
those who weren't priests or Levites, finally everybody, except the
high priest.

A holy God needed this kind of protection? No, he hadn't
wanted a temple in the first place. He made himself known without
walls, to a murderer as a burning bush in the desert, to anyone who
cared to look as a pillar of cloud or fire. His mission manifesto on
earth was to make the blind see, the deaf hear, the lame walk and to
free the prisoner—in a spiritual as well as physical sense. If all these
people would have been excluded from the temple as 'imperfect'
and 'unholy', how much more the riff-raff of society, the thieves and
prostitutes whom Jesus made his friends. Yet not only did he stay
pure and right before God, but many of them 'caught' his holiness.

The only temple Jesus inhabits is made of 'living stones'—imperfect
ones like you and me—and yet he is our glory within, he makes our
'city' holy. He's set us apart for him, yes, but has placed us in the
world which he loves. As we are touched by his holiness—and each
of our lives touch others—unwalled, we shine, like a beacon on a hill,
attracting people.

                                                              CL

Holiness beyond understanding

Nearby stood six stone water jars, the kind used by the Jews for ceremonial washing, each holding from twenty to thirty gallons.

From Noah onwards through history, drunkenness has spawned untold misery, violence, destruction and despair. So when the wine ran out at a wedding party, what on earth or heaven made Jesus turn perfectly good water into an over-the-top excess of 1,200 bottles (or thereabouts) of the finest Château Cana? I can't imagine—except that Jesus' presence always seems to make the unholy holy.

So do some people. When Stanley Spencer painted corners of junkyards or a grotesquely ugly couple in love he transformed both into something beautiful and compelling. 'I am always taking the stone that was rejected and making it the cornerstone,' he wrote. Spencer led a mixed up life, had some strange theology and I don't understand a lot of his work, especially where he seems to be equating sexual licence with heavenly holiness—yet as a friend said, 'He paints all those cavortings in such an innocent way. He doesn't *do* lewd!'

When my father-in-law was all tubed-up in hospital the week before he died of stomach cancer, nursing him can't have been at all pleasant. Pain-killing drugs left him barely conscious enough for communication, so there was no chance of the staff developing any real relationship with him as a human being. Yet the morning after he died, when we thanked the busy nursing sister for the wonderful way in which she and her staff had cared for him she said, 'It was a pleasure.' I don't know whether she's a Christian. But I saw in her eyes that she wasn't merely being polite, or resorting to a turn of phrase. This wasn't just another job to be done. Astoundingly, she meant those words. I glimpsed something of God's holy love then too.

Your holiness often surprises me, Lord. Help me reflect it as it is, not the way I, in my arrogance, think it ought to be!

CL

Beautiful in holiness

Therefore, as God's chosen people, holy and dearly loved,
clothe yourselves with compassion, kindness, humility,
gentleness and patience.

I started with questions: What is holiness and how can we be holy? Holy surely is what God is. His strength, integrity, love, joy, creativity and humour, his grace, goodness, generosity, greatness and compassion—his 'altogether loveliness'—is awesome to us.

Calling us 'holy and dearly loved', giving us himself, his presence, means holiness is where we start our Christian lives, not where we finish after years of self-denial and hard work. We are Cinderellas transformed into princesses; but there's one difference—though the ball gown's provided, no magic wand changes our clothes. We're to take off our dirty rags and put on the shining dresses provided! In dying, God's Son cleansed and enabled us to become his Father's holy children—and good parents long for their children to wear forgiveness rather than malice, love rather than slander. This holy clothing suits and is good for us, as well as pleasing to him.

I asked an elderly couple, who have joyfully served God all their adult lives, what they thought a holy person was. 'Consecrated, set apart,' they said but these 'theological' words suggest something stuffy, negative, unattractive—to me, anyway. 'You know a holy person when you meet one though, don't you?' The penny dropped. Yes, of course, people who remind me of Jesus, like this couple, who I'd guess don't think of themselves as 'holy'. I smiled, remembering this same elderly gent energetically careering around a chandeliered hall on one of those new scooter things. And in a creative writing group tasked with producing an article about the birth-control pioneer Marie Stopes, he was the only person who dared write about sex—a lively piece highlighting, with some humour, the positive (holy) nature of married love. Despite a stark, unloved childhood, he's allowed God to make him whole, loving, surprising, godly, good to be with, holy.

Thank you for the beauty of holiness—in yourself, Lord, in human saints, even in ourselves. May we choose to wear your bright clothes well!

CL

Psalm 37:1, 2 (NRSV)

Do not fret

Do not fret because of the wicked; do not be envious of wrongdoers, for they will soon fade like the grass, and wither like the green herb.

Are you envious of those who succeed through dishonest means? Those who get a good mark in exams, for example, because they have cheated, while you only scrape through after hours of hard work and swotting? Or those who get undeserved promotion, with a substantial raise, while you have trouble making ends meet? And in these days when violence and terrorism are rife, what is your attitude to the perpetrators of such wickedness? Perhaps you are being persecuted for your faith. What do you feel? How do you react?

This psalm repeatedly tells us not to worry and not to be envious of wrongdoers. As well as the above verse, we read in verses 7 and 8, 'Do not fret over those who prosper in their way, over those who carry out evil devices. Refrain from anger and forsake wrath. Do not fret—it leads only to evil'. Why shouldn't we be envious? After all, these people have everything going for them. It's not fair!

No, it is not fair. Neither is it the end of the story. David, the author of this psalm, sees beyond mere appearances and, in the face of human injustice, is glad to leave everything in the hands of a just God. He encourages us to do that too. We can so easily focus on our problems and on our material needs and desires, and so lose sight of the bigger picture. The psalmist makes it clear that evil men will not last for ever. They will fade and wither. 'The wicked shall be cut off' (v. 9). They 'will be no more' (v. 10). God who is sovereign and perfectly just will have the last word. For this reason we are told not to fret.

Never avenge yourselves, but leave room for the wrath of God; for it is written, 'Vengeance is mine, I will repay,' says the Lord.
ROMANS 12:19

BA

Trust in the Lord

Trust in the Lord, and do good; so you will live in the land and enjoy security.

Instead of being envious or jealous of wrongdoers and getting in a state because of wicked people, we are told in this psalm to do four things that will have positive consequences for us. Today we are going to consider the first of these: 'trust in the Lord, and do good'. This is the opposite to the evil men we read about yesterday, whose motivation is self-interest and who do wrong and carry out wicked schemes. As believers we are to 'trust in the Lord and do good'.

It is an exhortation that we find repeatedly in the New Testament as well. 'Bless those who persecute you... Do not repay anyone evil for evil, but take thought for what is noble in the sight of all', writes the apostle Paul to the Romans (12:14, 17). Jesus goes even further than that. He says, 'Love your enemies, do good to those who hate you, bless those who curse you' (Luke 6:27, 28). 'But that's not normal!' we might be tempted to exclaim. No, it is not something we would do naturally, but if we trust the Lord, he will give us the strength to put his teaching into practice. Jesus himself set us an example: 'When he was abused, he did not return abuse; when he suffered, he did not threaten; but he entrusted himself to the one who judges justly' (1 Peter 2:23).

Today's verse tells us that if we 'trust in the Lord and do good', we will 'live in the land and enjoy security'. We have here a picture of well-being, stability, peace, safety and fulfilment.

Lord, you know how difficult it is for us to face injustice. Our instinctive reaction is to hit back, to retaliate. We need a deep work of your Spirit within us to make us like Jesus. Help me to trust you, Lord, and to forgive, and to respond in love to those who abuse me in any way.

BA

My heart's desires

*Take delight in the Lord, and he will give you
the desires of your heart.*

We once had a wedding at our church at which five young girls called Jennifer were present! The bride's name was Jennifer, as was that of one of the bridesmaids. Some years before this happy event, Jennifer the bride had confided to one of the other Jennifers how much she wanted to find the man of her dreams and get married. The other Jennifer had pointed her to the above verse. The Lord did indeed graciously grant Jennifer's desire for a husband. At the wedding, this verse was printed on the order of service. The bride also requested that the sermon at the wedding service be based on the same verse.

When reading this psalm, it is very easy to pass straight to the second part of this verse: 'He will give you the desires of your heart'. We then conclude: 'Wow! That's great! God is going to give me everything I want!' Wait a minute. Is that what the verse really says? It is very easy for us to focus on our desires. But surely this verse is telling us that God is to be our focus. We have all that we need in him. Whether we realize it or not, I believe that he is the object of our deepest desire. We may only be conscious of our felt needs and desires, and we may not realize that Jesus is the One—the only One—who can meet our deepest needs. Surely once we come to understand this, then our deepest desire will be to know him better. It is only in him that we will find true fulfilment and satisfaction and meaning to life.

Thank you, Lord, that I have all that I need in you. Thank you for dying in my place and for saving me from sin. Thank you for the new life you have given me. I want to learn to put you first. I want to grow in my relationship with you.

BA

Hand it over

Commit your way to the Lord; trust in him, and he will act.

Are you perplexed about your circumstances? What a relief it is to know that God is in control, and that we can hand things over to him. We can leave everything in his hands. And what better hands could they be in than those of the almighty, sovereign God, who is also our heavenly Father who loves us and wants the best for us? The apostle Peter writes: 'Cast all your anxiety on him because he cares for you' (1 Peter 5:7). We sometimes talk about 'dumping' on people. Well, here we are invited to 'dump' on God.

Are you anxious about the future? You can seek God's guidance and direction. He will show you the way to go. He will keep you on the right road. 'If you wander off the road to the right or the left, you will hear his voice behind you saying, "Here is the road. Follow it"' (Isaiah 30:21 GNB).

Once again, in verse 5, as in verse 3 which we read a couple of days ago, we are exhorted to trust the Lord. The writer of the book of Proverbs says: 'Trust in the Lord with all your heart, and do not rely on your own insight. In all your ways acknowledge him, and he will make straight your paths' (Proverbs 3:5).

Our verse tells us that God does not remain passive. If we commit our way to him and trust him, he will act. He will meet our needs. He will lead us in the way we should go. Verse 6 tells us that bringing God into our situation, and doing what he wants us to do, will give us joy and peace of mind, which the psalmist likens to sunshine flooding our lives.

It reminds me of a little chorus we used to sing:

Heavenly sunshine, heavenly sunshine,
Flooding my soul with glory divine.
Hallelujah! I am rejoicing,
Singing his praises. Jesus is mine.
H.J. ZELLEY AND G.H. COOK

BA

Be still

Be still before the Lord, and wait patiently for him.

Be still. Calm down. Stop fretting. Stop fussing. Stop worrying. Stop getting in a state. 'Be still' could also be translated here, 'be silent'. On a TV quiz programme I saw recently, one of the candidates was asked if she was afraid of silence. She replied, 'Not at all. Silence is necessary for any deep reflection.' In our noisy world, where people seem to be always on the go, and where all around us horns blow and music blares and phones ring and electronic gadgets beep, it is not easy to find that quiet place to be still before the Lord, where we can learn to hand everything over to him and wait for him to act. Why not look for a place where you can spend time quietly in the Lord's presence?

'Wait patiently for him', says our psalm. Which of us likes to wait? Not very many people that I know! We are normally very impatient, but God will act, as we saw yesterday. God will act, yes, but when? In his own time—the right time, the best time. Whenever the Bible tells us to 'wait', it is never a passive resignation that is meant, but rather an active, eager, expectant anticipation.

It is still in the context of 'those who carry out evil devices', and who seem to succeed in everything they do, that the psalmist exhorts us not to get upset, but to 'be still before the Lord, and wait patiently for him'. If you follow the Lord, you will not escape suffering and injustice, but if you continue to trust him and hope in him and wait for him and hand everything over to him, you can be at peace, knowing that this all-powerful God, who judges justly, loves you and wants the best for you. You can count on him.

Wait for the Lord, and keep to his way, and he will exalt you to inherit the land.

Psalm 37:34

BA

Hope and inheritance

Those who wait for the Lord shall inherit the land.

The verse we concluded with yesterday (v. 34), as well as verses 9 and 11 which we are looking at today, all contain the same promise. The last three words in all these verses are indentical: 'inherit the land'. What land do they refer to? And who will inherit it?

I wonder if there is any thought in the psalmist's mind of the Israelites of old who, rather than wait for the Lord and trust him and expect him to act on their behalf, were afraid of giants, and refused to enter the land he had given them (Numbers 14:1–10)?

Verse 11 of our psalm tells us that it is the 'meek' who will inherit the land. Who are the meek? I think it is those we have been reading about over the past few days who, rather than act aggressively out of anger and a spirit of revenge, trust in the Lord and take delight in him, those who commit their way to him, who are still before him and wait for him. The wicked will disappear (v. 10), leaving the meek to take possession of the land. Jesus used this same expression in the Beatitudes, where he says, 'Blessed are the meek, for they will inherit the earth' (Matthew 5:5).

Have we taken possession of all that God wants to give us in Jesus? Many times in the New Testament, we read that we are 'heirs' of God, 'heirs of the kingdom that he has promised to those who love him' (James 2:5), 'heirs of the gracious gift of life' (1 Peter 3:7). We can look beyond all the injustices of this world, sure of our inheritance in Jesus Christ.

Blessed be the God and Father of our Lord Jesus Christ! By his great mercy he has given us a new birth into a living hope through the resurrection of Jesus Christ from the dead, and into an inheritance that is imperishable, undefiled and unfading, kept in heaven for you.
1 PETER 1:3–4

BA

Deliverance

The salvation of the righteous is from the Lord; he is their refuge in time of trouble. The Lord helps them and rescues them; he rescues them from the wicked, and saves them, because they take refuge in him.

Having considered the four exhortations that will have positive consequences for us if we heed them: 'Trust in the Lord, and do good' (v. 3); 'Take delight in the Lord' (v. 4); 'Commit your way to the Lord' (v. 5), and 'Be still before the Lord and wait patiently for him' (v. 7), we now move on to more words of assurance and encouragement, as David brings his psalm to a close. Salvation is from the Lord, and the righteous look to him to be their refuge and their deliverer. He protects them and rescues them. There is no longer any need to fret and fuss. They find all that they need in God.

Who are the righteous? Doesn't the Bible say, 'There is no one who is righteous, not even one' (Romans 3:10)? Yes, it does. It also states that God 'made him to be sin who knew no sin [Jesus Christ], so that in him we might become the righteousness of God' (2 Corinthians 5:21). I am a sinner. I deserve to be punished for my sin. 'The wages of sin is death', writes the apostle Paul (Romans 6:23). However, Jesus died in my place. He paid the penalty. God now sees me as righteous in Christ. So, declared righteous, I can claim these promises in Psalm 37.

What about you? Have you accepted God's gift of salvation in Jesus Christ? Is he your refuge in times of trouble? Do you experience his help and deliverance? Have you discovered that God can meet all your needs?

As you take refuge in the Lord, as you trust him and do good; as you delight yourself in him; as you commit your way to him; as you are still before him and wait patiently for him, may you find him to be your deliverer, your stronghold, your help and your salvation.

BA

Ephesus 1

'I know your works, your toil and your patient endurance. I know that you cannot tolerate evildoers; you have tested those who claim to be apostles but are not, and have found them to be false. I also know that you are enduring patiently and bearing up for the sake of my name, and that you have not grown weary.'

Revelation is a difficult book to understand. It was written at a time when the Christians were suffering persecution because they would not submit to the annual ritual of acknowledging Caesar as a god. The events in Revelation are written in a code that the contemporary readers would understand, but the authorities would not. Even if we do not know the exact meaning of this code, we can still gain much encouragement from the book; especially the letters dictated by the risen Christ to the seven main churches in Asia Minor at the time.

At the beginning of this letter, Christ praises the Ephesians for their toil, and their steadfast endurance. The word used for toil implies the kind of effort into which someone has put all their physical and mental energy; it is not a half-hearted, self-pitying effort. It is the kind of effort that Paul indicates when he says, 'I will most gladly spend and be spent for you' (2 Corinthians 12:15). Even in the most demanding of situations, such as the ever-present threat of physical danger combined with the mental and spiritual fight against false doctrine, the power of God's Spirit enables us to 'withstand on that evil day, and having done everything, to stand firm' (Ephesians 6:13b).

The patient endurance that the Lord praises here is not grim resignation, but the kind of perseverance that produces the image and character of Christ in us, that turns suffering and hardship into grace and glory (1 Peter 4:12–13).

Lord, thank you that we are completely in your grip, and that you will never let us go. When times are difficult, physically and mentally, give us the strength to continue, and the mind to lean only on you.

AS

Ephesus 2

'But I have this against you, that you have abandoned the love that you had at first. Remember then from what you have fallen; repent and do the works you did at first. If not, I will come to you and remove your lampstand from its place, unless you repent.'

The way that Jesus speaks to the church at Ephesus is a model we can use when we talk to those who are precious to us: emphasize something positive first, to make the negative thing that follows easier to bear. After emphasizing their hard work, endurance and testing of false teachers, Jesus gently points out that the Ephesians have abandoned the love they had at first… let anyone who has an ear listen to what the Spirit is saying to the churches.

This might mean that they had lost the enthusiasm and devotion that they had when they first came to know the Lord (cf. Jeremiah 2:2), that their faith had become dull, routine and lifeless with the passage of time; passing not into mature, faithful commitment, but indifference. It could also mean that they had spent so much emotional and intellectual energy in testing the teaching of those claiming to be apostles, that they were now wrung out and cynical, unable to open their hearts to one another due to suspicion, wounding and exhaustion. Whatever the cause, the Lord called them to remember, repent and return.

When I asked Jesus into my heart as an 11-year-old girl my love and my faith were uncomplicated and childlike. With the passage of over 30 years and all that has encompassed and entailed, both good and bad, I am wondering if I still have retained that childlike quality in some corner of my heart, or has it been squeezed out? What about you? Jesus calls us to remember, repent… and return; his arms are open wide.

Lord, help me remember the way I used to love you. I repent for the fact that I have made love conditional and complicated. Forgive me and draw me back into the joy of your salvation. Amen.

AS

Smyrna 1

*'And to the angel in the church in Smyrna write: These are the
words of the first and the last, who was dead and who came to
life: "I know your affliction and your poverty, even though you
are rich. I know the slander..."'*

Smyrna was a city in Asia Minor only second in importance to
Ephesus, but it was the first to have embraced worship of the Roman
emperor and was the home of a large part of the population that was
hostile to the Christian church. Most of the Christians were among
the lower classes of society and often suffered for lack of food. They
suffered further hardship when mobs attacked their homes and
spoiled their goods.

The risen Jesus says to these afflicted people that he *knows* what
they are suffering and he *knows* about their poverty. The kind of
poverty that is being described here is not just the lack of anything
beyond the bare essentials, but negative equity and destitution. To
add to this, the Christians were being slandered; many of their practices were misunderstood and it was not difficult for malicious people to spread gossip about them. Jesus says he knows about their
situation, but despite their afflictions they are rich—having nothing, but possessing everything (2 Corinthians 6:10)—because of
what the Lord has done for them. This is part of God's upside-down
economy and the apparent contradiction in terms that can be found
in the Christian faith: the poor are rich, the weak are strong, the
first will be last, and so on.

I take great heart from the words in this letter, because our house
was recently stoned, our net income decreased below our regular
outgoings, and I heard some terrible things said about members of
our family. But the Lord *knows* about all these things, and he is the
unchangeable reference point by which we should measure our
outer circumstances.

---

*Thank you, Lord, that whatever we go through or are threatened
with, you are not ignorant of it—you know—you care—and you provide all our different needs according to your riches in glory. Amen.*

                                                                    AS

Smyrna 2

*'Do not fear what you are about to suffer. Beware, the devil is
about to throw some of you into prison so that you may be tested,
and for ten days you will have affliction. Be faithful unto death
and I will give you the crown of life... Whoever conquers will not
be harmed by the second death.'*

In the latter part of the letter to the Christians at Smyrna, John
prophecies that they will be imprisoned. The phrase 'for ten days' is
not literal, but means 'for a short time'. What might seem to be an
encouragement in saying the imprisonment is to be short, is more of
a warning. Then the only release from imprisonment for Christians
was execution; Smyrna was the city in which the bishop Polycarp
was burnt to death for refusing to curse Christ and sacrifice to
Caesar.

Jesus speaks into the situation and describes himself to them as
'the first and the last' (1:17). This is how the Lord God described
himself in the Old Testament (Isaiah 44:6–8), there is none like him
from everlasting to everlasting, and his people are exhorted not to
be afraid. Yet this everlasting God allowed himself to become the
one 'who was dead and came to life'. God himself had identified
himself with human suffering and death, yet had risen to life again.
In the human form of Jesus, he experienced the depths of human
suffering, but is alive. No matter what happened to the Christians in
Smyrna, they were assured that one had gone before them, had conquered the worst that humanity could experience and offered the
way to victorious living.

The crown that is promised to the one that endures to the end is
not a royal crown, but a crown of joy and victory that permits the
wearer to enter the presence of Almighty God and sit at the wedding feast of the Lamb.

---

*In this life it may be that a Christian's loyalty will bring [her] a crown
of thorns, but in the life to come it will bring [her] the crown of glory.*
WILLIAM BARCLAY

AS

Pergamum 1

*'These are the words of him who has the sharp two-edged sword.
I know where you are living, where Satan's throne is. Yet you are
holding fast to my name, and you did not deny your faith in me
even in the days of Antipas my witness, my faithful one, who was
killed among you, where Satan lives.'*

The risen Jesus is addressing the Christians in a city which was a centre of pagan worship, both Greek and Roman. The Roman governor of the town was one of those who had been granted to bear a double-edged sword. This meant he had the power to execute a person on the spot, and the Christians were at the mercy of his whims. Yet, Jesus assures them that he knows where they are living. Like the Christians in Smyrna, their situation is known to the living God who cares for them like a father.

The original word for 'living' is interesting, because it implies permanent rather than temporary residence. These Christians were long-term inhabitants of the city, not just passing through. This is significant, because the level of insidious threat and open persecution that they faced was enough to have driven them to find a new place to live. But they stayed, even when one of their number, Antipas, was killed—tradition has it that he was slowly roasted alive inside a brass bull.

It would be very unusual for any Christian in the West to be faced with such covert or overt danger, but when we find things tough, we often think it's time to move on rather than time to dig in for the long haul. Jesus, the one who has the two-edged sword, reminds us that it is he who ultimately has authority over life and death and bids us not to be afraid but depend on him.

Thank you, Lord, that you have the ultimate authority in our situation. There is no one else we can depend on but you; you have the two-edged sword—the words of eternal life that lead us in to all truth. Amen.

AS

Pergamum 2

'I have a few things against you: you have some there who hold to the teaching of Balaam... So you also have some who hold to the teachings of the Nicolatians... To everyone who conquers... I will give a white stone, and on the white stone is written a new name that no one knows except the one who receives it.'

It may be one thing to make a conscious decision to stay and serve the Lord in a situation that is dangerous and difficult, as opposed to running away, but it is quite another to try and remain 'separate' from the situation. The constant nagging on the emotions can start you thinking that little compromises won't really matter. The trouble with little compromises is that they breed constantly bigger compromises until people suddenly find they are not 'separate' any longer, but have moved slowly and imperceptibly into the ranks of the majority they had initially intended to distance themselves from.

The Christians in Pergamum had compromised by eating food sacrificed to idols and by indulging in sexual self-indulgence. The names 'Balaam' and 'Nicolatians' come from the Hebrew and Greek words, 'to conquer the people'. If the Christians in Pergamum did not actively refrain from the eating of meat offered to idols in contexts where immoral sexual activity often ensued, they would become 'a conquered people', no longer living under the sovereign rule of Christ, but under the rule of the pagan influence of the surrounding society.

Jesus promises that to all who stand firm and conquer he will give a white stone inscribed with a name (v. 17). The long-serving Roman gladiator, who lived long enough to earn honourable retirement, was given a white stone bearing the letters SP (*spectatus*—a man whose valour has been proved beyond doubt). Jesus promises his 'conquering heroes' in the arena of life a token allowing them to enter heaven with honour if they continue to stand in difficult circumstances.

What is the equivalent of 'meat offered to idols' in your situation? Will it lead you to greater compromises? Ask the Lord what he wants you to do about it.

AS

Thyatira 1

'These are the words of the Son of God, who has eyes like a flame of fire, and whose feet are like burnished bronze: "I know your works—your love, faith, service and patient endurance... but... you tolerate that woman Jezebel... she refuses to repent of her fornication... I am the one who searches minds and hearts, and I will give to each of you as your works deserve. But to the rest of you... only hold fast to what you have until I come."'

Thyatira was not a place where Christians were under threat of persecution, but the commercial status of the town meant that to succeed in business one had to belong to a trade guild or association. These associations often held feasts in which meat offered to idols was eaten, and behaviour descended into a drunken orgy. To cut oneself off from membership of a guild was to commit financial suicide for the Christian businessman or woman of the time. It was quite a dilemma.

Jezebel, whether this was her actual name or not, had dressed her arguments up in spiritual language and was persuading the Christians that it didn't matter to associate with the guilds and adopt their practices. It is not clear whether her fornication (v. 21) is 'spiritual' (cf. Mark 8:38) or 'actual'; but spiritual adultery would inevitably lead to actual adultery in the situation at Thyatira. Jezebel's motives were compromising and self-seeking for her own financial gain.

Sometimes we need to make decisions that may be seen as suicidal in relation to our career or business prospects, and that is difficult. We might think we can hide our compromises beneath a veneer of Christian behaviour (cf. v. 19), but we should remember that Jesus sees through our schemes and strategies with eyes like flames of fire. Jesus Christ demands a pure heart and right motives from those who call themselves his, no matter what the cost.

You desire truth in the inward being; therefore teach me wisdom in my secret heart. Purge me with hyssop, and I shall be clean; wash me, and I shall be whiter than snow.

PSALM 51:6

AS

Thyatira 2

*'To everyone who conquers and continues to do my works to the
end, I will give authority over the nations... even as I also
received authority from my Father. To the one who conquers I will
also give the morning star. Let anyone who has an ear listen to
what the Spirit is saying to the churches.'*

As with the letters to the other churches we have read so far, continuing and conquering in Christ are the things every Christian is
urged to do. In a sense they are dependent on each other. We need
to conquer ourselves every moment in order to be faithful and continue in our walk with Christ, and we need to continue, i.e. persevere, in order to attain the final conquest or victory—a life lived
wholly for him until we meet him in heaven. We can only continue
and conquer by depending on Jesus every step of the way, because
we do not have the strength to achieve this without him—we live
for him and through him—holding fast to what we have until he
returns (v. 25).

To those that are faithful Jesus promises 'authority over the
nations' (v. 26) or similarly, the 'nations [as] your heritage' (cf.
Psalm 2:8). The risen Jesus has immovable power, as symbolized by
the description of his feet as being like burnished bronze (v. 18). He
is the one who bears ultimate authority over the peoples of the
earth, despite the Christians in Thyatira feeling that they were in
the power, and at the mercy of, the pagan trade guilds.

When Jesus was tempted in the wilderness, he was offered all the
nations of the world if he, Jesus, would bow down and worship the
devil (Luke 4:5–7). Jesus countered the temptation by reminding
the devil that we should 'worship the Lord your God, and serve only
him'. Authority is not ours to take, but as in Jesus' case, given only
as a result of submission to the will of God and of perseverance and
obedience to suffering—continuing to the end.

---

*Bright and Morning Star, may you yourself light our way and be our
reward.*

                                                                  AS

Sardis 1

*'These are the words of him who has the seven spirits of God and
the seven stars: "I know your works; you have a name for being
alive, but you are dead. Wake up and strengthen what remains
and is on the point of death, for I have not found your works
perfect in the sight of my God. Remember then what you received
and heard; obey it and repent."'*

Sardis was a city in which the Christians did not face persecution
from any quarter. The city itself had once been wealthy and powerful but was now in decline, lifeless and indifferent. In this atmosphere the Christian church had sunk to the level of the community
in which it lived; it was a church in name only—doing enough to
remain 'active', but insufficient to draw attention to itself by living
out the radical claims of Christ. In effect the church was dead; it was
'holding to the outward form of godliness but denying its power' (2
Timothy 3:5).

Spiritual death and sin are often likened to each other. In 2
Timothy 3:2–4 Paul lists many of the sins that lead to spiritual indifference and the refusal to allow the Holy Spirit's power to move in
our lives. In today's passage, Jesus calls to those of us who have
allowed ourselves to fall into indifference and sin to wake up while
there is still time, repent and strengthen what remains. We need a
fresh touch of the Lord's forgiveness and healing power to help us
'rekindle the gift of God that is within us… for God did not give us
a spirit of cowardice, but rather a spirit of power and of love and of
self-discipline' (2 Timothy 1:6–7).

Christ who speaks to the church at Sardis and has the seven spirits of God—the completeness of the Spirit—reminds us we need
complete filling to finish the task he has set before us.

---

*Lord, help us to remember what we received and heard when you first
met with us, and kindle it to life again. Amen.*

AS

Sardis 2

*'If you do not wake up I will come like a thief, and you will not
know at what hour I will come to you… [those] who have not
soiled their clothes; they will walk with me, dressed in white,
for they are worthy. If you conquer, you will be clothed
like them in white robes…'*

Twice in its history, the besieged city of Sardis fell because the people were not watching. The people were so confident that their citadel city was impregnable that the sentries on night duty did not stay at their posts; this gave the enemy troops the chance they needed to scale the only crack in the rock face and conquer the town. It might be understandable for this to happen once… but twice? You would think they would remember the weak spot and defend it!

Yesterday we saw how the Christians in Sardis had become over-confident and indifferent; only having the outer form of religion. In today's passage, Jesus tells them to be alert, to watch, because they do not know the hour he will come and hold them to account. He wants to find them *all* worthy to walk with him in the kingdom of heaven wearing the white robes that symbolize victory, purity, resurrection and the assurance of a place at the feast of the Lamb, that is Christ.

If they are to be found watchful and prepared for the Lord, they also need to be watchful for their enemy, the devil, who is constantly prowling round ready to strike unawares. Similarly we need to be aware of the cracks in what we might consider our otherwise unassailable citadel that might be used as a foothold for the devil when we are not expecting it. It has been said that constant watchfulness is the price of liberty. We have been given liberty in Christ, but the price is that we need to be constantly looking out for the potential pitfalls that lie in our path, guard against them… and learn from our mistakes!

In you, O Lord, I seek refuge; do not let me ever be put to shame.
PSALM 31:1

AS

Philadelphia 1

*'These are the words of the holy one, the true one, who has the
key of David, who opens and no one will shut, who shuts and no
one opens: "I know your works. Look, I have set before you an
open door, which no one is able to shut."'*

When Jesus speaks to the church at Philadelphia he first describes
himself as 'the holy one and the true one'. 'Holy' is the description
of the Almighty God, who is separate and different from human
beings (read Isaiah 40:25), and implies that the risen Christ shares
the being of God. 'True' here implies 'real', as opposed to the opposite of false. When confronted by the risen Lord we are confronted
with the reality of who he actually is and what he has won for us in
the heavenly realms. It might be good to take a moment to let the
depth of this sink in.

When Jesus describes himself as having the key of David, this is
a metaphorical way of showing the degree of *authority* that the
Father has given him (see Philippians 2:9–11). The description
relates to Eliakim, the faithful servant of the Old Testament king
Hezekiah, who was the only person who could give someone access
to the king. By his death, Jesus has opened the door that gives us
access to the kingdom of heaven so that we might stand blameless
before the Father, King of kings and Lord of lords. No one can shut
this door; Jesus has opened it once and for all, all we need to do is
accept the invitation to step through it (Hebrews 4:16).

The open door can also be symbolic of the opportunities the Lord
has opened up for us to walk into. Philadelphia lay on the borders of
three countries and was in a prime position for missionary opportunity. Jesus is encouraging the Christians there to rise to the opportunity despite their apparent weakness and the potential opposition.

---

*Is there an open door of opportunity that the Lord has set before you?
What prevents you walking through it?*

AS

Philadelphia 2

'Because you have kept my word of patient endurance, I will keep you from the hour of trial that is coming on the whole world to test the inhabitants of the earth... If you conquer, I will make you a pillar in the temple of my God; you will never go out of it. I will write on you the name of my God...'

What is 'the word of patient endurance' that the Christians in Philadelphia have kept? Back at the end of verse 8 we see that they have kept his word and not denied his name. The verbs here imply an act that happened one time in the past; therefore the Christians have had to make a stand over an important issue from which they have emerged faithful and true, despite their little strength. But it appears that the tough times are not over. Jesus warns them that a time of trial will soon face the whole world, but because they have been faithful in this incident in the past, the Lord with give them the strength to be faithful in the difficult times to come.

What were the difficult times that were coming? It seems to me that the influence of other 'modern' religions was to be a major challenge to the churches in Asia Minor. When the six other cities fell to the power of Islam, Philadelphia endured until the 14th century, and even then maintained a Christian church in otherwise occupied territory.

In our postmodern culture, where pluralism is quietly gaining an increasing foothold, it is becoming more and more difficult for the committed Christian to stand up and be different, because we are allowing ourselves to become submissive to the all-embracing spiritual atmosphere of society around us.

But the Lord calls us to be 'separate' and different. He promises that those who endure, who conquer will be pillars in the temple of God, inscribed with his name; i.e. they will stand in his presence for ever, marked out as having been faithful to him in their life time on earth.

Lord, help me to stand and dare to be different. Amen.

AS

Laodicea 1

'I wish you were either cold or hot. So, because you are
lukewarm, and neither cold nor hot, I am about to spit you
out of my mouth. For you say, "I am rich, I have prospered,
I need nothing." You do not realize that you are wretched,
pitiable, poor, blind, and naked.'

Laodicea is the only church about which Jesus has *nothing* good to say. The place itself was a banking and financial centre, one of the wealthiest cities in the world, a producer of fine black woollen tunics, a centre of healing and the location of warm mineral springs. The city was proud of all these things, rich and self-sufficient, with no need of outside support. The Christians there had allowed themselves to become immersed in this atmosphere and had been dragged under by it.

The writer of Proverbs prays fervently that God will allow him to be neither rich nor poor, for if he becomes rich, he might deny and curse his God (Proverbs 30:7–9). It seems this is what had happened to the Christians in Laodicea; they had become materially rich and indifferent to God. Jesus uses the image of the Laodicean hot springs to illustrate this; the warm, mineral rich water would make the drinker sick to the stomach—this is how Christ felt about these Christians.

The Laodiceans were proud of their black woollen garments, but Christ tells them they are spiritually naked; they are proud of the eye salve they exported, but Christ tells them they are spiritually blind. He encourages them to come to him for true riches—faith tested by the crucible of experience, for white robes—the inner beauty that only Christ, by his grace, can give; and to come to him for eye salve—healing for their spiritual sight, so they could see themselves as they truly were and repent.

It is never easy to look at ourselves as God really sees us—it takes true humility, but the Lord honours that humility with his lovingkindness and all-embracing forgiveness.

Lord, I come to you just as I am… refine, heal and clothe me.

AS

...odicea 2

*...iscipline those whom I love... Listen! I am
...door, knocking; if you hear my voice and open the
...ome in to you and eat with you, and you with me. To
the ...who conquers I will give a place with me on my throne...'*

Despite the words of praise, the risen Jesus has had many difficult words to say to the members of these seven churches. But here we meet words of encouragement... the Lord only disciplines those whom he loves, and the word for 'love' here has the most tender connotations. Despite all their faults, these Christians are incredibly precious to the Lord and the rebuke that he gives them is not intended for condemnation, but to enable them to see their mistakes and put things right (Psalm 94:12). It is more of a punishment for the Lord not to intervene in a person's life!

The Lord who loves us tenderly is knocking at the door of our hearts seeking admission. The Christian faith is unique in this respect; no other religion has a God that actively seeks to dwell in the hearts of human beings. Love can go no further than the Almighty God reaching down from the heavens to bring the people he created and loves back to himself without any effort on their part except to acknowledge his reign in their lives.

The opening of the door of the heart to Jesus is the responsibility of each individual—no one else can do it on our behalf. Yet when we admit Jesus into our lives he, as promised, enters in and eats with us. The resultant fellowship we have with Jesus, the metaphorical meal described here, is not a quick snack or a working lunch, but a lingering evening meal in which the participants rejoice in the pleasure of each other's company.

Lord, thank you that the messages of these letters still speak to our hearts and lives today. Help us to hear what your Spirit is saying to us as individuals and as churches. Amen.

AS

Unexpected upheaval

'You will be with child and give birth to a son, and you are to give him the name Jesus'... 'I am the Lord's servant,' Mary answered, 'May it be to me as you have said.' Then the angel left her.

What a tremendous upheaval in Mary's young life! We bring some upheavals upon ourselves by the decisions and choices we make—changing jobs, having babies, moving house or, like me, emigrating! But this dramatic upheaval in Mary's life came out of the blue. She had just been living her life as a normal Jewish girl and was preparing for marriage, when suddenly the angel's message turned her life upside-down.

Her response is a lesson in trust and humble acceptance of God's perfect plan. She recognized her place before God, which was as a servant—she was not calling the shots, God was. He had revealed his plan to her and she said, 'OK, the consequences of this event are in your hands. Use me as you will.' God must have been thrilled with that attitude.

No doubt as the months and years went by she had to keep reaffirming her trust in God as she faced becoming an unmarried mother, the trauma surrounding her son's birth, watching him grow up, develop as an adult, leave home, become this amazingly popular teacher and healer, then suffer a humiliating trial and agonizing death.

What about us? When changes, not of our own making, are thrust upon us, do we recognize that God is ultimately in control? When life keeps springing surprises on us, do we keep going back to God, trusting his ways and not our own wisdom? Proverbs 3:5–6 sums it up: 'Trust in the Lord with all your heart and lean not on your own understanding; in all your ways acknowledge him, and he will make your paths straight.'

Help me, Lord, to remember that you are the boss and I am your servant.

                                                                    CP

An enemy attack

*Sarai ill-treated Hagar; so she fled from her... She [Hagar] gave
this name to the Lord who spoke to her: You are the God who sees
me, for she said. 'I have now seen the One who sees me.'*

Hagar got a pretty raw deal. She had to sleep with her boss's husband, so when she became pregnant she took the opportunity to get
back at her boss. Things went from bad to worse... so she ran away.

Verse 7 reveals God's compassionate heart. An angel of the Lord
found Hagar and spoke to her. Hagar realized that even though
she'd been treated unfairly God was still concerned about her. The
paraphrase of Romans 8:28 could be her theme song: 'The Lord may
not have planned that this should overtake me, but he has most certainly permitted it. Therefore though it were an attack of an enemy,
by the time it reaches me, it has the Lord's permission and therefore
all is well. He will make it work together with all life's experiences
for good.'

Where is God when upheavals are thrust upon us like an attack
of an enemy? His promise is that somehow in the end he will bring
good out of it.

God chose not to rescue Hagar from her plight. She still had to
go back and submit to Sarai, who was no doubt still angry. But she
had God's promise that he did know what was going on and he had
plans for her life and for her unborn son.

I often wish that God would change my circumstances and make
life cosy and comfortable. I struggle against pain, disappointment,
seeing others suffer, and general hassle! But, like the weaver with a
tapestry, the black threads are just as important as the gold ones.

---

*Lord, just as Hagar obeyed you and went back and submitted to
Sarai, please help me see you in my own particular wilderness. Enable
me to face my life circumstances, knowing that you are with me and
care deeply for me.*

CP

Into an unknown future

But Ruth replied, 'Don't urge me to leave you or to turn back from you. Where you go I will go, and where you stay I will stay. Your people will be my people and your God my God. Where you die I will die, and there I will be buried.'

Naomi had tried to persuade Ruth to stay in her own country where she'd be secure and safe and probably find another husband. That made logical sense… but not to Ruth. She'd come to know the God of Israel and didn't want to remain in her pagan homeland. She was also intensely loyal to Naomi and wanted to support her on her long journey back to the land of her birth.

So she chose the path of the great unknown. There is an excitement in starting new adventures, but it is also quite scary. Frodo in *The Lord of the Rings* was really a home bird. He loved the Shire but chose to follow his destiny and go on a quest to destroy the Ring. Like Ruth he had no idea of what lay ahead—some wonderful experiences, some terrifying ones, but both of them stuck with it. In this reading Ruth reveals her absolute determination to accompany Naomi. There is nothing wishy-washy about her. She has made her decision and will not turn back no matter what happens. She has left herself no get-out clauses.

I'm sure Ruth had to keep reaffirming her commitment as she faced challenges in her new country. It is good that we don't know all the details of what the future holds—some of us might be too daunted to get out of bed in the mornings!

All our major choices have unknown consequences—the only one who knows what is going to happen is God—and he is good and wise.

You will keep in perfect peace him whose mind is steadfast, because he trusts in you.
ISAIAH 26:3

Lord, help me to trust you even when my choices don't turn out the way I'd hoped.

CP

Facing bad news

*Even in darkness light dawns for the upright... He will have no
fear of bad news; his heart is steadfast, trusting in the Lord.*

A friend of mine is trying to cope with the aftermath of some very
disturbing news. A Christian she trusted has been revealed to have
been living a double life, and several people have been damaged
emotionally as a result.

God does not expect us to sail through these experiences on a
fluffy pink cloud. This is devastating. It is a betrayal of her trust and
friendship and in that sense it is like bereavement—something that
she held as precious is no longer there. In times like this we may
experience similar feelings as a bereaved person—denial, shock,
anger, and eventually acceptance and resolution.

It is important not to minimize or trivialize the pain, but allow
the grieving process to take its course. There are no pat answers to
dilemmas like this—all we know is that God is still on the throne.
He is the Judge, he is the Healer. He is the One who will give stability and peace even when the news is very bad.

In my friend's case other Christians are coming together to pray
and to support each other—the result of which is deeper relationships than before as they grapple with disappointment, incompre-
hension and hurt. The church leaders have shown themselves
willing to confront the person concerned and deal thoroughly with
all the after-effects. This has also led to the church members having
a greater respect for and confidence in their leaders.

This psalm talks about the person 'who fears the Lord, who finds
great delight in his commands'. Those who love God and who want
to live lives that honour him will find his word and his Spirit are
their refuge, no matter what ghastly news drops in through their letter box or down their phone line.

---

*Lord, I can't deny that some events really trouble me. Please help my
heart to be steadfast, trusting in you.*

                                                                    CP

Joyous upheaval

I prayed for this child, and the Lord has granted me
what I asked of him. So now I give him to the Lord…
My heart rejoices in the Lord.

Some changes are wonderful! Any parent knows that after the birth of a child life is never the same. Their newborn infant is precious and unique, even though to others' eyes he/she may be indistinguishable from any other baby!

Hannah had agonized in prayer for a child and Samuel was eventually born to her. He brought huge joy to her life. She had to adjust her lifestyle to meet his needs—she experienced many changes. Her attitude in facing this beautiful change in her life was one of worship. She recognized that God had given the child. She took no credit for herself. She thanked and honoured God—the Holy One, the Rock (2:2). This enabled her to offer Samuel back to the Lord for his service. It's not surprising that Samuel grew up to be a godly man and was widely used by God as a judge in Israel.

All Christian parents have to trust God for their children, but Hannah had to do it at long-distance. The only way she could continue to influence her son was by prayer and perhaps by annual visits.

When God has answered my prayers and good things have happened, I find that my prayers of thanks can sometimes be a bit sketchy. I quickly pass on to the next prayer request. I'm guilty of being like the nine lepers who didn't turn back to thank Jesus for their healing (Luke 17:17). When he enables me to do well in anything it is tempting to think that my gifts have contributed to the success.

Hannah pours out her love and thanks to her Lord. Her prayer is recorded for ever in God's word to us. I can't imagine God recording any of my prayers to pass on to succeeding generations!

Lord, help me to be more like Hannah, and truly to thank and praise
you for all your great goodness to me.

                                                                    CP

Resistance to change

*Ahab told Jezebel everything Elijah had done and how he had
killed all the prophets with the sword… Jezebel sent a messenger
to Elijah to say: May the gods deal with me… if by this time
tomorrow I do not make your life like that of one of them.*

Ahab had returned home bursting with the news of what had happened on Mount Carmel—how the priests of Baal had been completely defeated; how the God of Israel had hurled down fire from
heaven to burn up the sacrifice; and then how, in answer to Elijah's
prayer, it had begun to rain again after a drought lasting three years.

You'd think that a dramatic demonstration of power like that
would cause anyone to reconsider their convictions. But not Jezebel.
Whatever God did, she was not going to turn away from worship-
ping Baal. She would not bend the knee to the God of Israel. To
prove it, she threatened his servant, Elijah, with death.

She was resistant to any change God wanted to bring into her
life. She paid dearly for this. She remained unrepentant and met a
horrible death (2 Kings 9).

God uses the image of the potter and the clay when speaking
about the moulding he wants to do in our lives. The clay needs to
be soft and malleable, sensitive to the gentlest touch of the potter's
hands. It is not up to the clay to decide what the pot should be like
(Isaiah 64:8).

What makes us resistant to change? Fear of failure, fear of the
unknown, fear of getting out of our comfort zone, pride—being
unwilling to admit we are wrong? Resisting God will impoverish our
lives. Allowing him to lead us into new adventures will be scary and
exciting. What could be greater than co-operating with the God of
the universe in his mighty plans?!

There is no fear in love. But perfect love drives out fear, because
fear has to do with punishment (1 John 4:18).

---

*Lord, I offer myself to you. Help me see when I'm resisting your touch
on my life.*

CP

Final change

*Dear friends, now we are children of God, and what we will be
has not yet been made known. But we know that when he
appears, we shall be like him, for we shall see him as he is.*

One day, maybe soon, Jesus will return to earth. Archangels will
shout, trumpets will sound. Christians who've died will rise first and
then believers alive on earth will go up to meet Jesus in the clouds!
(1 Thessalonians 4:17). At that point we will be changed to be like
him—imagine that—like Jesus!

All memory of sin will be erased. We will be pure and holy. We'll
have new resurrection bodies (1 Corinthians 15:51–54)—all aches,
pains, sickness, tears will be abolished for ever (Revelation 21:4).
What a magnificent future ahead of us. So, how should we prepare
for this final change?

- Be ready to meet him at any moment. Jesus said, 'Yes, I am coming soon.' Our response: 'Amen, Come, Lord Jesus' (Revelation
  22:20). Yes Lord, I'm ready for you to come right now. Let's not
  allow sin to fester, but confess it as soon as we are aware of having
  blown it.
- Hold lightly on to the things of this world. Let's not be consumed
  with possessions or worldly ambitions, but have our hands open so
  that God can take or give as he chooses.
- Be ready to talk about Jesus with anyone who's asking questions.
  We can be a light in the darkness and show people the way to God
  so they too can share in this glorious future. If we don't, the alter-
  native is too awful to contemplate.
- Make the most of each day. Living with regrets or hankering after
  the past is futile. Putting today on hold and focusing on future
  events, such as when I get married, or when I've finished my
  course, is also futile. Let's live in the reality of meeting Jesus face
  to face in the next few minutes.

---

*Lord, use this day to prepare me a little more for heaven. Please help
me see opportunities to speak about you and to show your love to
those around me.*

CP

Being right

Again, the gift of God is not like the result of the one man's sin:
The judgment followed one sin and brought condemnation, but the
gift followed many trespasses and brought justification. For if, by
the trespass of the one man, death reigned through that one man,
how much more will those who receive God's abundant provision
of grace and of the gift of righteousness reign in life through the
one man, Jesus Christ.

It's time for a deep breath as we dive headlong into Romans for the next few days. As we follow Paul's train of thought through the middle chapters of his remarkable letter, I am hoping that some of his excitement and conviction will seep into our understanding of the gospel and set it alight. A glance at Acts, or at any of Paul's letters, shows us a man who lived and breathed the gospel. He could not stop communicating it to others, despite frequent opposition. We all know about his Damascus road experience (Acts 9), but perhaps Romans reveals more than any other letter just what that event did to his theology, and therefore to his life.

We're leaping in a third of the way through the letter. Previously, Paul has been setting out the case for faith. He has reminded us that we are all sinners under the judgment of God. We need the righteousness Jesus gives us when we believe in him. We cannot be right with God through our own efforts, nor through our attempts to keep the law. We can only be declared righteous by faith.

So far, so good. Now Paul reminds us that, as usual, God's grace-filled response to our predicament totally outweighs the problem. His extravagant response brings life and abundant provision that makes the original evil look paltry. God has not grudgingly let us off the hook. He has gone over the top in grace. We are not just delivered from the deathly wage of sin, but given life, grace and righteousness before God—all as a free gift.

What does the gift of righteousness mean to you?

DA

Doing right

What shall we say, then? Shall we go on sinning, so that grace may increase? By no means! We died to sin; how can we live in it any longer? Or don't you know that all of us who were baptized into Christ Jesus were baptized into his death?... Count yourselves dead to sin but alive to God in Christ Jesus.

Paul seems to think of every possible objection to his argument and tackle it head on. I think arguing with Paul would be no easier than arguing with a 21st-century teenager. There is no way out.

Here, Paul defends his argument about grace against those who might accuse him of encouraging sinful behaviour. If God's response to our sinning is so wonderfully full of grace, then how about we sin more so we can have more grace? That may sound ridiculous, but haven't we come across the oh-well-never-mind-God-will-forgive-me-anyway attitude? Even in ourselves?

Perhaps Paul knew that he was not just playing with words here; perhaps he spotted this attitude in Christians around him. His answer is to remind us forcefully that if we want the life Jesus offers, then we have no option but to die to sin. Baptism into Christ Jesus means leaving the old behind and counting it dead.

I don't know about you, but I reckon this is easier said than done. Even when we get the hang of Paul's logic and agree with him completely, even when we are passionate about being alive to God, death still comes hard. Sometimes sin still looks so appealing and we want to revive the old self enough to indulge. Sometimes we forget that in so doing, we actually miss out on grace, and cannot look God in the eye. Not to mention the utter mess that sin drags in its wake. Is putting to death the bits that drag us down really such a high price to pay?

Read Mark 9:43–50.

Dear Father, thank you that you understand our struggles. Please give us your power to make choices for life. Amen.

DA

Who is your master?

Do not offer the parts of your body to sin, as instruments of wickedness, but rather offer yourselves to God, as those who have been brought from death to life; and offer the parts of your body to him as instruments of righteousness. For sin shall not be your master, because you are not under law, but under grace.

Who is your master? Obviously those of us who are Christians want God to be, don't we? We want to offer ourselves to God whole-heartedly, and shun sin.

Why then does Paul feel it necessary to spell out the mechanics of our salvation? Why does he go to such lengths in Romans to hammer home the implications of Jesus' death and resurrection for our daily lives? Experience suggests that it is because we need telling. Our redeemed humanity still needs reminding over and over again about grace. Because of grace, we can stand tall before our Father God, and walk forward in his unconditional love. But we have tried to be righteous—to get it right—all by ourselves, and tied ourselves in extraordinary knots in the process.

I am constantly amazed at the new levels of sin I discover in myself. I can be incredibly creative at living without trusting God completely. Despite my mental assent to Paul's words, I can still hold back from letting God's grace loose in my life. What a waste! What happens to my theology? Do I forget who God really is? Do I doubt that he has my best interests at heart? Have I still not under-stood the message of grace?

'We creatures, we jolly beggars, give glory to God by our dependence. Our wounds and defects are the very fissures through which grace might pass. It is our human destiny on earth to be imperfect, incomplete, weak, and mortal, and only by accepting that destiny can we… receive grace. Only then can we grow close to God.'
PHILIP YANCEY, *WHAT'S SO AMAZING ABOUT GRACE?*, ZONDERVAN, 1997

How about a verse of 'Amazing Grace'?

DA

I do...

So, my brothers, you also died to the law through the body of Christ, that you might belong to another, to him who was raised from the dead, in order that we might bear fruit to God... For what I do is not the good I want to do; no, the evil I do not want to do—this I keep on doing.

It all makes such good sense: if we leave one master and submit to another, then the latter master will be our boss. We die to the power of sin and law, and become alive to Jesus, and sin no longer has mastery over us. Sorted.

So why does Paul write his famous 'I do what I don't want to do' bit? Apparently, mighty theologians have wrestled over this passage for centuries. Is Paul writing from a Christian or pre-Christian point of view? How can there be a struggle with sin if we are saved from it? Perhaps he is talking about Israel? It would be lovely to solve this long-running debate here, and confound the great and good—but perhaps not. While the argument rages on, it seems to me nothing compared with the tussle that Paul describes. Because we Christians *do* battle with sin. That is how it is. We want to 'bear fruit to God', but it seems extremely hard at times. Sometimes the power of sin breathes down our necks and distracts us from our wonderful God and all our good intentions. Sometimes it even laughs in our faces as we hit the dirt again.

How do we escape? How do we keep standing against temptation? Perhaps a good place to start is to confess to each other how hard we find the battle. The truth is that we have all sinned. It has to be better to fight this thing together, than struggle alone. Like sportswomen need coaches, we need each other to pick us up and cheer us on when the going gets tough. Let's dare to be real together and force sin into retreat.

Read 1 John 1:5—2:2.

DA

Freedom!

Therefore, there is now no condemnation for those who are in Christ Jesus, because through Christ Jesus the law of the Spirit of life set me free from the law of sin and death. For what the law was powerless to do in that it was weakened by the sinful nature, God did by sending his own Son in the likeness of sinful man to be a sin offering.

OK, now for the good news. If you have been following Paul's line of argument, then the claims of these verses are pretty amazing. Sit down with a cuppa and read the whole letter of Romans so far to get the full impact of what Paul is saying. Romans can be hard-going because of Paul's insistence on covering all his bases. But it is worth getting the hang of his theology, because it is life-changing.

Probably none of us are going to take issue with Paul on this 'no condemnation in Christ Jesus' bit. We have heard it quoted many times. We understand that Jesus took the punishment we deserved, and are profoundly grateful. We know that the law did not save us, because we tried to be perfect on our own and it didn't work. But here comes the challenge: Are we *living* as if there is no condemnation?

> 'We read, we hear, we believe a good theology of grace. But that's not the way we live. The good news of the Gospel of grace has not penetrated the level of our emotions.' (David Seamands, 'Perfectionism: Fraught with Fruits of Self-Destruction' in *Christianity Today*, 10 April 1981)

How can we allow the good news to permeate our thinking and our feeling? How can we walk through this world in such a way that others covet our freedom? What about all that negative stuff that drags us down—why should we miss out on an iota of what Jesus has achieved for us? We must learn together what it means to live in freedom.

Dear Father, help me to experience daily the freedom you have given me. Amen.

DA

Spirit life

You, however, are controlled not by the sinful nature but by the Spirit, if the Spirit of God lives in you... But if Christ is in you, your body is dead because of sin, yet your spirit is alive because of righteousness. And if the Spirit of him who raised Jesus from the dead is living in you, he who raised Christ from the dead will also give life to your mortal bodies through his Spirit, who lives in you.

It just gets better and better. The great thing about Paul's logic is that it is a real help on those days when everything seems wrong and the probability of God existing is very small. Or is it just me who has days like that?

But I love the way that one thing follows on from the last with Paul, so the truths are entwined. If on my somewhat blank days I can get hold of just one of them, then all the others follow behind. So this reminder that Christ lives in me by his Spirit means that I have him on my side for fighting off the old sinful stuff. AND it means that though my body is still paying the duty for sin, my spirit is not going to die because Jesus is alive. AND it means that even my body will get another chance and be part of the resurrection. AND it means that life now is full of possibilities because that amazing Spirit lives in me... My goodness, I nearly cheered myself up there with the thought!

Seriously, this is mind-blowing. When was the last time you stopped to enjoy the fact that the same Spirit who created the world lives in *you*? How can we give ourselves space to savour our special relationship with God? The demands of every day and the ups and downs of life can easily squeeze out the opportunity to enjoy our Father in heaven. But why should we miss out?

What are the best ways for you to make the most of this amazing relationship with God?

DA

Daddy

... those who are led by the Spirit of God are sons of God.
For you did not receive a spirit that makes you a slave again to
fear, but you received the Spirit of sonship. And by him we cry,
'Abba, Father.' The Spirit himself testifies with our spirit
that we are God's children.

I know, I know. All this talk of 'sons' doesn't feel very female, but that's not the point. Take it as a generic term and don't worry about it—after all, Paul does use the word 'children' as well. Perhaps this is one occasion when we want to be sons anyway, because they were the ones in Paul's day who inherited the best of everything. The sonship Paul refers to carries the idea of adoption, and adopted children in Greek and Roman times were granted the full privileges of a natural child. Our future is secure because we belong.

I reckon this is the sort of passage to meditate on, and commit to memory. How often do we give in to thoughts of shame and unworthiness? How often do we fear we don't really belong because we are not nice/pretty/clever/together enough? How often do we worry that no matter how hard we try, we will never really please God? Compared to the truth of this passage, and the truth we know in our heads—that Jesus died for us and that's all it takes—we know our fears are invalid. But I sometimes wonder if the unfinished nature of many women's lifestyles unsettles our security in God. There is always more to do, isn't there? More washing, more shopping, more caring, more planning, more juggling diaries, more working, more bringing up children... always more.

Paul's point is that no matter what our lives consist of, we belong to God. We can even use that extraordinarily familiar term 'Abba', or 'Dad', when we talk to him. We can be free from fear when we remember that.

Dad, help me to enjoy the freedom of being your child today. Amen.

Read Isaiah 49:15–16.

DA

Backup

*I consider that our present sufferings are not worth comparing
with the glory that will be revealed in us… In the same way, the
Spirit helps us in our weakness. We do not know what we ought
to pray for, but the Spirit himself intercedes for us with groans
that words cannot express. And he who searches our hearts knows
the mind of the Spirit, because the Spirit intercedes for the saints
in accordance with God's will.*

It is good to look forward and know that one day all the struggling
will be over. 'You've only got to keep it going for so many years,' says
my sister. 'Then we get the glory.' Which is a relief really. Even
though I am not sure what glory looks like.

'In the same way,' says Paul, we get help now too. It is not just
'pie in the sky when you die'. It is very much 'steak on your plate
while you wait'. (Actually I'm a vegetarian so I need a rhyming alter-
native. 'Ratatouille' doesn't have the same ring…) We are not
alone! The Spirit begs and pleads and prays for us. Isn't that great?
He prays for us wholeheartedly—he puts everything into praying for
us, even groaning. Can you imagine the Spirit of God praying for me
and you with such intensity that he can't even find the words?
Incredible. He prays in our *weakness*—for all those things that we
find most difficult about life, and about being who we are. What
extraordinary backup! He is there, all the time, praying about the
things that need it most, and getting it right because he is God.

I trailed round the streets today after my son who had left a vital
schoolbook at home. He was suitably grateful—wise child. He will
thus escape punishment from his tutor. I wonder, when we finally
discover what glory looks like, will we also learn how the Spirit rescued us from trouble with his prayers? Is it time we relied a bit more
on the enormity of his support?

Read John 17:6–26.

DA

Romans 8:28–29 (NIV)

The God who acts

And we know that in all things God works for the good
of those who love him, who have been called according to his
purpose. For those God foreknew he also predestined to be
conformed to the likeness of his Son, that he might be the
firstborn among many brothers.

Hands up all those who have had this verse slapped like sticking-plaster over the pain of intolerable situations by well-meaning fellow Christians! In times of confusion and hurt, it is often extremely hard to see God at work and I have often wished heartily that this verse were the other way round. If only it said, '*In all good things* God works for those who love him'. Wouldn't it be great if we were promised only good things because we love Jesus?

Paul knew better than most that being a Christian does not vaccinate you against bad times. Indeed, it was after he met the risen Jesus that his troubles really started. His evangelistic zeal was not only rewarded by new converts and churches, but also by persistent persecution and orchestrated opposition. By the end of his life, he had acquired a list of adventures and hardships that would put James Bond to shame. Yet still Paul could record his confidence that in all of these things, God was working for his good. He was convinced of the security of his calling as a child of God. His life had purpose, and God was making him more like Jesus every day.

It is tough to hang on to this perspective when life is hard. But it is either true or it isn't. If God is who he says he is, then troubles are not going to stand in the way of his plans. This is also, of course, incredibly comforting if it is we ourselves who have caused the distress. When we have blown it single-handedly, it is great to remember the 'all things'. Clearly God can take anything and work it into his good plan for us. The challenge is, will we let him?

Read 1 Thessalonians 5:16–18.

DA

Certainty

*And those he predestined, he also called; those he called, he also
justified; those he justified, he also glorified. What, then, shall we
say in response to this? If God is for us, who can be against us? He
who did not spare his own Son, but gave him up for us all—how
will he not also, along with him, graciously give us all things?*

There almost doesn't seem any point writing about these verses.
They seem to me the sort that we need just to read again and again
till they have sunk in properly. Then we can go on our way rejoicing at their incredible truths.

Is there anything about those verses that you have trouble believing? Is there anything you don't understand? I can see that the predestination bit might cause a hiccup because it is another of those
things that theologians have disagreed on for centuries. While I am
totally committed to the necessity of good theology, I think arguing
about it is a waste of time. We could be out there being witnesses for
Jesus and watching him bringing folk into relationship with him,
rather than discussing how he does it. Our friends are only going to
be interested in how it works for them. Do you know how you would
describe your journey to Jesus to someone who wants to hear?

Apart from predestination then, any other problem? Do you
know you are called, justified, glorified? Do you understand it? Do
you believe that God is *for* you? Do you feel it and live it? Do you
trust that God will give you 'all things' you need for your faith walk
to end in unqalified success?

No wonder Paul had the confidence to zip around the
Mediterranean with the good news. No wonder he got up again and
carried on after every beating, imprisonment, shipwreck and
snakebite. No wonder he planted all those churches. He knew what
his relationship with God meant.

---

*Dad, please help me to understand and live by the amazing things you
have done for me. Amen.*

DA

Separation

For I am convinced that neither death nor life, neither angels nor demons, neither the present nor the future, nor any powers, neither height nor depth, nor anything else in all creation, will be able to separate us from the love of God that is in Christ Jesus our Lord.

Here we go again. Another phenomenal statement from Paul that doesn't need me to add to it. Perhaps the best thing would be to write out the above verses for yourself and stick them on the kettle, or somewhere else you will see them frequently. Feel free to put this book down now and let Paul's words revolutionize you.

Of course nothing can separate us from God! Why would he go to all that trouble to rescue us, and then let something come in the way? That would not make any sense at all!

So why do we doubt it? Why do we not always stride in confidence through the day, knowing that God is on our side, and nothing can come between us and him? Once when I was horribly ill, I convalesced at my Mum's. I was desperate to hang on to God in a difficult time, but he got smaller as the illness got more painful. Finally he was a distant pinprick of light, almost eclipsed. For years afterwards I raged against that abandonment, wondering how others managed to experience God so closely in times of pain. Finally I came to see that of course God was still there, no matter how I felt. The truth was that I was cared for, my family coped without me, I did get better eventually, and my Mum was wonderful to me. I had to learn that God was there even when it didn't look or feel as if he was. I then realized I had felt the same sense of loss on other occasions, which sent me on a journey back to my childhood, and to the subsequent discovery that God can deal with the past, as well...

Nothing can separate us from the love of God.

DA

Paul and Israel

I have great sorrow and unceasing anguish in my heart.
For I could wish that I myself were cursed and cut off from
Christ for the sake of my brothers, those of my own race,
the people of Israel. Theirs is the adoption as sons; theirs the
divine glory, the covenants, the receiving of the law,
the temple worship and the promises. Theirs are the patriarchs,
and from them is traced the human ancestry of Christ,
who is God over all, for ever praised! Amen.

These verses follow straight on from Paul's stirring proclamation about the security of our relationship to God which we looked at yesterday. I can't help speculating as to the link here—for pages and pages Paul has elaborately defended the Christian faith. He ends with that wonderful triumphant air-punching shout of conviction that is now stuck to your kettle. Then suddenly it hits him again— his fellow Jews are left out. It feels like a blow to the stomach as Paul attempts to express the genuine agony this causes him.

Much of his thesis has been based on the very things that he lists here—the law, the promises, the covenant relationship with God. Without these we would not have understood our need for a saviour. Yet the very people through whom God brought these things were not responding to the good news of Jesus. Paul was in the minority among the Jews. Of course there were many Jewish believers, but the leaders of Judaism had spurned Jesus and were now rejecting Paul. Israel was turning away.

No less real is the pain we feel when friends and family do not understand our faith, and reject its message. We long for them to experience the reality of Jesus alive today, but they don't want to know. Would we trade our salvation for theirs, as Paul expresses? Do we allow the pain of others' ignorance of God to touch us, and fuel us to pray? Can we ask God for a renewed compassion for those we love who do not know him yet?

Read Matthew 18:12–14.

DA

Grace again

Israel, who pursued a law of righteousness, has not attained it.
Why not? Because they pursued it not by faith but as if it were by
works... at the present time there is a remnant chosen by grace.
And if by grace, then; it is no longer by works; if it were grace
would no longer be grace.

There are good days when the world is in glorious colour and we feel
so close to God we can almost touch him. We vow we will never feel
faithless again. We cannot understand why the whole world is not
Christian when the truth of Jesus is so utterly obvious, and makes
such sense.

Oh come on, there are times like that, aren't there? Paul must
have had loads of them—after all, he even heard Jesus' voice and
went down under that blinding light. To a man of such conviction
and intelligence as Paul, that Israel as a nation was rejecting Jesus
must have been excruciatingly difficult. His conclusion is sober-
ing—it was because the Israelites couldn't receive the message of
grace. They just couldn't let go of the works thing—they wanted to
earn their way to heaven.

We are back to grace again, then. How many times have you
heard a preacher point out that Christianity is the only religion that
does not demand we sweat and strive our way to bliss? How ridiculous that God has done it all for us. But before we look at all the
other 'isms' and feel smug, what about that grace thing? Since we
came across it last week, have you grown in your understanding of
it? Has it changed your thinking? Are you living in it a bit more?
Paul keeps going back to grace again and again. He stresses that it
is what the good news is all about. The only reason he and some
Jews *are* Christians is because of grace. They are the remnant God
has always kept for himself.

Can you ditch a few 'should-must-and-ought's today and live in
grace?

Read Jeremiah 23:1–4.

DA

Why, Lord?

Again I ask: Did they stumble so as to fall beyond recovery? Not at all! Rather, because of their transgression, salvation has come to the Gentiles to make Israel envious. But if their transgression means riches for the world, and their loss means riches for the Gentiles, how much greater riches will their fullness bring!... Israel has experienced a hardening in part until the full number of the Gentiles has come in.

The question of why Israel as a whole did not accept Jesus as their long-awaited saviour has vexed many minds. Part of the answer Paul found was in the consequent benefit to the Gentiles. Because the Jews so thoroughly persecuted Christians, the latter were forced to flee and thus took the good news with them to the Gentiles. Paul himself spent much of his life telling the Gentiles about Jesus. In the above passages, he expresses his conviction that the eventual blessing for both Jews and Gentiles would be worth the cost of the current Israelite rejection of Christ. Israel's turning away was for the benefit of the rest of the world.

We too have unanswered 'why's?' in our lives that we struggle with. All of us have things we wish had not happened, which were unfair, which threatened to destroy us, and which continue to haunt us. Despite Paul's confident assertion of benefit to the Gentiles, there were still millions of Jews who never knew that Jesus was their Messiah. There still are. Sometimes we just have to live with the questions.

I listened the other day to someone talk about their missionary parents. This person knew that her parents had been instrumental in bringing help and salvation to hundreds of people. But she herself felt abandoned because she was sent away to England to boarding school and did not see her parents or siblings for years. She felt she bore the cost of her parents' calling. She admitted there were no easy answers. It felt very similar to what Paul says about Israel.

Dad, help me to trust you even when there are no answers. Amen.

DA

Roman praise

*Oh, the depth of the riches of the wisdom and knowledge of God!
How unsearchable his judgments, and his paths beyond tracing
out! 'Who has known the mind of the Lord? Or who has been his
counsellor?' 'Who has ever given to God, that God should repay
him?' For from him and through him and to him are all things.
To him be the glory for ever! Amen.*

Did Paul write this letter himself, or dictate it? I like to think of him
dictating it, pausing here from his concentrated pacing up and
down, and flinging his arms around a bit as he attempts to capture
for his readers the incredible nature of the God we have. Paul does
have a way of summing up the good stuff.

After all his exhaustive theology, Paul just has to put in a bit to
remind us how amazing it all is. Isn't it great that God's ways are not
like ours, and we don't fully understand them? If we did, he would-
n't be God, would he? He knows what he is doing—he is in control.
He knew what he was going to do about the human predicament
right from the start, and he can be trusted to see it through to its
conclusion. He is so big! Everything depends on him—not just us.
And there's that grace again—Paul reminds us we cannot give anything to God, to make him owe us something. We just live in and
enjoy his glory!

Paul clearly loved to express himself in words, but we may be different. Got an idea for a picture or a song? Fancy a solitary walk to
revel in creation, or a noisy praise session with some friends? How
can we show praise of God today? How can we live as if all the above
is true? It doesn't matter how, but let Roman theology permeate
your doing and being.

Dad—I want to stand tall
  Walk in confidence
    Act in freedom
      Enjoy grace
And be with you today.

Read Jude 24–25.

                                                          DA

DAY BY DAY WITH GOD

MAGAZINE SECTION

Prayer gates	136
Mountaineering	140
Body building	143
(Extra) Ordinary Women	147
Other Christina Press titles	152
Other BRF titles	154
Order forms	156
Subscription information	158

Prayer gates

Celia Bowring

Lift up your heads, O you gates; be lifted up, you ancient doors, that the King of glory may come in. Who is this King of glory? The Lord, strong and mighty, the Lord mighty in battle. Lift up your heads, O you gates; lift them up, you ancient doors, that the King of glory may come in (Psalm 24:7–9).

Sometimes I go sailing with my brothers. Their boat is kept at Birdham Pool, an idyllic spot in Chichester Harbour walled off from the rest of the tidal waters so that it stays at the same level. Birdham is sheltered from the wind and waves, with food, fuel and other supplies on hand as well as people who can carry out repairs and give friendly advice. I love its quiet, restful atmosphere—especially after returning from a stormy trip out to sea, cold, wet and longing for food and respite from the weather.

We can't simply sail into Birdham Pool at any time, though. We have to pass through the lock, which has watertight gates at each end to separate the variable tidal waters outside from the constant higher level within. When he sees us coming, the lock keeper pumps out some water from inside the lock, and once the level is down to where we are, waiting on the outside, he opens the gate. We enter the lock, he seals the gate behind us and lets enough water gush back in to float us some five or six metres up to match the level of the Pool inside. And then the inner gate opens to admit us to the still water within.

Access to God

Going through Birdham Lock makes me think about how we gain access to God, our heavenly Father. His presence is like an unfailing refuge, somewhere aside and apart from the difficulties and uncertainties of life. The only way in is by Jesus, who laid down his life for us. There he is at the gate, pouring out the living water of the Holy

Spirit to bring heaven down to us and us up to heaven. Without him it is impossible to rise from the low, muddied streams of our world up into the pure waters of his grace. He opens the 'strait gate' of salvation and lets us in. In fact, Jesus actually called himself a 'door'—although he was thinking of us as sheep rather than sailing boats! (John 10:7).

All of us who trust in Christ are welcome to come in and out of God's presence whenever we wish, so why is it that I'm sometimes reluctant to stop and spend time praying and praising him? Perhaps it seems too much of an effort and I feel I've got to struggle against the prevailing winds and tides of my own selfishness to find the way in. Perhaps the tide feels too far down, and there is something between God and me—disappointment, unforgiveness, fear or sin.

When I became a Christian, I was really fortunate to meet a group of mature and dedicated believers who took me under their collective wing and helped me to understand my faith and grow as a child of God. One thing that they really stressed was the importance of a regular 'quiet time' of prayer and Bible study. 'It's a sort of gateway,' they explained. A bit like Birdham Pool Lock, I supposed.

But alas, as a typical free-spirited child of the do-your-own-thing '60s, not raised in church and endowed with rather a butterfly mind, I found this discipline impossible. It just wasn't me. My conversion had been a passionate discovery of the grace of God that made me want to serve him for ever, but I was a bit lazy and easily distracted. I did love to sing to God, spent ages writing poetry and walked for hours enjoying just 'being', pouring out the way I felt and owning up to my resentments and fears. Quite often, circumstances I had asked him about changed in quite remarkable ways. But to my mind I was clearly useless at praying and lived in a semi-permanent state of guilt because I could never keep up my daily devotions. I was also constantly torn between pretending I did and confessing I didn't. As president of my college Christian Union and then, at the age of 21, a pastor's wife, I usually succumbed to the first option, and this hypocrisy made me feel even worse.

Communication

It seems obvious to me now, some thirty years on, that prayer is far bigger than one way of doing it. Prayer is the communication that takes place because of my relationship with God, and this is expressed and achieved in countless ways. If I were to list ways I communicate in my human relationships, I'd need a large piece of paper. Some ways, I'm better at than others. Birthday cards are a disaster. I don't much like the phone unless it's someone I know and love very much or there is a clear important reason for ringing. But give me some peace and quiet to write a letter or the opportunity for relaxed conversation and I am in my element. (The problem always seems to be finding the peace and quiet.) I realize now, it's exactly the same with God and me. I wish that early on someone had encouraged me more to push open all those windows of my emotions, intellect and creativity to begin to develop my own unique prayer life.

The presence of God is lurking around every corner of our being. He wants us to push open the gates and come on through. But more profound still is to understand the truth that he has come to dwell in us! Those wonderful verses of Psalm 24 speak of how the cross of Jesus, the strong and mighty King, triumphed over the devil and removed the offence of sin so that the ancient doors separating us from a holy God could now be lifted up. Communication with God does not involve complicated ritual or strict ways of doing it because he is nearer to us than breath itself. Through gates of thanksgiving, appreciation, joy, pain, creativity, selflessness and praise, we're right there with him.

I am still searching and learning to discover a fully-orbed and balanced prayer life. It is challenging, but I thank God that it is not something I feel guilty about any more. Most days now I do enjoy a quiet time. I snuggle under my duvet with my one-year Bible and a mug of tea and muse for a while, drifting in and out of words as I think of certain people and situations. On my ten-minute walk from the tube station I almost always pray for the members of my family, each by name and sometimes in some detail. In the car I often sing. Sometimes I weave language together to create the combinations of words that I need to shape my prayers but other days I am dumb and just hope to catch a whisper of comfort or guidance. I am beginning to understand that God's presence is not something I have to get into, but it is Birdham Pool, my mooring, the place where I am. And even when I do have to venture out into rough water, he is there in the boat with me and around me.

Pray thoroughly

What about you? I am convinced that many others struggle as I do to pray more, pray thoroughly and in a way that fits who I am. Are you clanking about in Saul's armour (just like the boy David when he was given someone else's equipment to fight Goliath) when in your pocket you have the familiar and effective sling and five stones? Think about the ways in which you communicate best, the unique means by which you express who you are, and see how to transfer them to your spiritual life. It should be natural—although often needing determination and courage, discipline and being stretched. But of course this freedom is inextricably bound up in the truth of the Bible. There may be many means but there is only one way in to meet with God, and it is through the narrow passage of salvation that Jesus admits us each time.

So if you ever find yourself going into Birdham Pool, or in a boat through any other lock, for that matter, smile at the friendly face of the weather-beaten lock keeper. Let him remind you of another Gate-keeper, always there to welcome us through another Door that was once lifted up in love and grace.

Celia Bowring is the compiler of CARE's *Prayer Guide* which highlights family and community issues. Her book *The Special Years* is for parents of children under five. She works closely with her husband, Lyndon, in CARE, and is a contributor to several periodicals.

Mountaineering

Sandra Wheatley

There is the faintest possibility that I may soon ascend the dizzy heights of Mount Snowdon in a powered wheelchair! The logistics of transporting me and a support team from the north-east to Wales are posing one or two problems, but I'm game for it and looking forward to attempting to 'climb' a mountain once again.

It is one thing I do miss since becoming a wheelchair user—hiking, fell-walking, rock climbing, being out and about in the glorious countryside. Sadly, fells and mountains are not the most accessible places. But I do have wonderful memories of the mountains I have climbed and the days spent alone walking the fells of Upper Teesdale and the Lake District.

There are a few references to mountains in the Bible and as Christians we often see a 'mountain-top' experience as being one of joy and victory—even though the process of getting there can be arduous. Moses saw the burning bush on Mount Horeb; he received the Ten Commandments on Mount Sinai. Elijah challenged the prophets of Baal on Mount Carmel, and Jesus was transfigured on Mount Hermon and ascended from Mount Olivet. Incredible and amazing things happen on mountains! No wonder we favour a mountain-top experience rather than a 'valley' experience.

Yet not all the stories relating to mountains are pleasant. On Mount Moriah Abraham was willing to sacrifice his beloved son, Isaac. What a time they must have had as they journeyed. Modern-day 'mount' Moriah is apparently the site of the Temple Mount in Jerusalem and has the Dome of the Rock built upon it. It doesn't look much like a mountain in comparison to some of the others but it will still have posed quite a challenge to a young boy like Isaac. The Bible tells us that Abraham and Isaac spoke as they journeyed—mainly about the provision of the lamb for sacrifice. All the while, Abraham encouraged his son to keep on going, that God would provide.

Encouraging

The last time I was able to climb Helvellyn in the Lake District, I took my younger brother along with me. He was ten years old at the time. I had climbed it many times; this was to be his first and last! I had to keep encouraging him to continue as he asked how much longer it would be before we reached the top. 'Just over the next ridge,' I would reply... and three hours later we arrived. The view was stunning and I was thrilled. My brother looked around for the transport that he hoped would take him down. I hadn't told him that the only way down was the way we had come up. I wonder if Abraham had to encourage Isaac along in the same way!

A little while ago, in the midst of a rather nasty relapse, I felt as if my body was closing down on me. System by system, things were being affected by the MS—my kidneys, my lungs, and my eyesight. I felt in a sorry state.

The minister from my church, Paul, and two elders came to pray with me. When I spoke about feeling as if my body was closing down, Paul told me of a book he was reading about mountaineering. Apparently, on an ascent of Everest there is a recognized portion of the climb that is called the 'Death Zone'. Because of the altitude and lack of oxygen, the body begins literally to close down. The climber needs to make a decision: abandon the climb and come down the mountain, or continue with the aid of oxygen.

Whether or not my circumstances were the 'Death Zone', I wasn't sure. One thing I did feel was that it didn't seem to be my time to continue the metaphorical ascent up this mountain.

Praying

Before he prayed, Paul read a scripture to encourage us to believe the Lord for healing. I giggled as he read from Luke 9: the passage he read began, 'The next day when they came down the mountain...' Paul hadn't chosen those verses for the reference to mountains, but it helped me to know that I would indeed be coming down this particular one.

The Lord of the mountains is also the Lord of the valleys. Some of the lushest vegetation grows in the valley, and some of our deepest and most life-changing events happen as we walk through the valley—even the valley of the shadow of death.

So it was as I came down from my latest 'mountain'. During my sojourn in this recent valley I came to a point of utter desperation and during one particular difficult time echoed the words that Elijah spoke in 1 Kings 19: 'He came to a broom tree, sat down under it and prayed that he might die. "I have had enough Lord," he said. "Take my life...".' I had been given a course of intravenous steroids in an attempt to kick-start my body into action, but it was evident quite quickly that they had not had the desired effect. Things worsened at an alarming rate and I was on a rollercoaster ride of pain and emotional turmoil, culminating in a weekend where I didn't think I could carry on. I wouldn't ever consider taking my own life—but I did beg God to let me die!

Thankfully, friends from church responded to my pitiful cries for help. They prayed with me and drew alongside. The following day in church, the congregation joined in a concerted prayer for this weary little life. The Lord heard and answered and in the days that followed I was able to find my harbour of acceptance again.

One song has kept coming back to me and shows just what a difference he does make in our lives. The song? 'Take my life and let it be consecrated, Lord, to thee'. What a turnaround with the same words. Weeks ago, 'Take my life' was said out of desperation. Today I say it with devotion.

Body building

Angela Griffiths

Have you ever given much thought to body building? I don't mean the kind of thing that happens in a gymnasium, lifting weights and suchlike; I mean something much more important and lasting. It does not cost anything in terms of money. It only requires a sensitive heart, a caring attitude, and the willingness to co-operate with God. What I'm talking about is the building up of the Church, the body of Christ. One way to achieve this is by the ministry of encouragement.

Encouragement is needed very much in our churches today, and not only in our churches but in our communities too. As life becomes more fast and furious, there are people all around who feel excluded, discouraged and generally out of step. But with God's help, we can make a difference. We can show the compassion of Christ and give the encouragement that will enable a person to keep going. We can encourage those who are full of faith as well as those with little or no faith. When the right opportunity presents itself, we can gently encourage people, young or old, to discover their individual gifts and develop as Christians.

The gift of time

In our church or any other situation, God will help us to know what form our encouragement can take. Perhaps all that's needed is a smile and a few friendly words, or perhaps we can pass on a book or a cassette tape we've enjoyed. We can ask God to bring to our attention anyone who would welcome a visit or an invitation to tea or coffee. This would mean the gift of our time, a precious commodity these days. But there are people who need to talk and be listened to. Can we fill that need?

About seven or eight years ago, I was at a week-long conference in Derbyshire. During one lunch hour I went for a stroll in the beautiful grounds of the conference centre. As I walked, I was thinking about the Association of Christian Writers, of which I am a member. What our Association needs, I thought, is someone to whom members can write when they need advice or prayer support, someone to whom they can turn in times of trouble or when they just need a friend who will empathize and encourage.

A few steps further on, another thought came to me, and it was just as if God had tapped me on the shoulder. 'You could be that person,' he seemed to say. I stopped in my tracks, full of self-doubt. Then I walked on again, and within a few minutes the idea seemed less daunting. After all, I knew about the ups and downs of being a writer and I was a trained counsellor. Added to that, I'd always enjoyed writing letters. By the time my walk was over, I had made a decision. If it was God's will, I'd be happy to do it!

Soon after that, I got in touch with the committee of our Association, and I was delighted when they welcomed and approved my proposal. I served as the official Encourager for just over four years, during which time I answered hundreds of letters and prayed daily for members with specific needs. During those years I learnt a lot. I found that the more I encouraged others, the more God encouraged me. It was a tremendous time of blessing all round. The Association now has a successor Encourager—an excellent one, I might add.

Used by God

In the book of Acts we can read about Barnabas, who was called the 'Son of Encouragement'. Barnabas was a church leader who befriended the newly converted Paul and stood by him when others were still wary because of Paul's past history. From our vantage point now, we can see that the help given by Barnabas to Paul had important and far-reaching effects. It led to the establishing of many new churches; it also led to Paul becoming a dynamic leader who was used by God for the spread of the gospel.

We can learn a lot from Barnabas. He was a generous man of faith and courage. We may not be able to show generosity in the way that he did (he sold land and gave the money to the apostles, Acts 4:37), but we can always be ready to give our friendship and ongoing support. If we take Barnabas as our role model, we will see what it means to be an encourager. It means being willing to recognize and promote the talent of others while taking a back seat yourself.

It means being patient, available for the long haul. It means wanting to be useful rather than wanting to be noticed. All this might sound quite alien in today's highly competitive culture, but for the true encourager it will mean deep joy.

As Christians, our chief desire is for God's will to be done. We will be ready to encourage anyone who comes to us, not too concerned with a person's church affiliation or whether they worship in the same style as us. Whether they are high church, low church, or no church, we will only want to help and to show the love of Christ.

Last year a dear friend of mine died after a long illness. I visited her in hospital the day before she died. I sat by her bedside and held her hand. Then she mentioned the title of her favourite hymn. I managed to quote the words of the first verse of the hymn (I could only remember that one verse) and we spoke quietly about the meaning of the words. She smiled, squeezed my hand, then drifted off to sleep, and it was obvious that she had been encouraged. This was a new experience of encouraging for me. It was difficult because of the sadness involved, but God was clearly in it.

Encourage one another

We can see from Paul's letters to the churches that he repeatedly urged both leaders and new believers to encourage one another. In Acts 20, we read of him speaking many words of encouragement to people as he travelled. In his letter to the Romans he looks forward to the time when he and the church members will meet and be mutually encouraged by each other's faith (Romans 1:11–12). Perhaps you can recall times when your faith was strengthened by the words or actions of another Christian. I know I feel grateful for the many times I have been helped by others on my spiritual journey. I recall two particular periods in my life when I felt profoundly grateful for the help given by women of faith.

Look around your church. Is there someone who needs your encouragement? Is there someone who would be strengthened by a genuine 'thank you'? Is there someone newly bereaved who needs a word of comfort? Is there someone coping with divorce or family problems, or someone struggling with feelings of failure or rejection? A few kind words given at the right time can make all the difference. Most people don't need advice, and certainly not our criticism. What most people want to know is that we are there for them.

They need to know that we genuinely care, and are willing to pray for them. Daily prayer support means a lot to someone who is struggling through a dark patch.

One day we ourselves might be in need of encouragement. I wonder what sort of encourager you would want? What qualities would you look for? I think my ideal encourager would be a caring, sympathetic, sincere person who prays and who truly loves God.

In the book of Hebrews the first-century believers were told to encourage one another daily. So now let me encourage you, and myself, with the timeless words of Jesus Christ.

'Come to me, all you who are weary and burdened, and I will give you rest. Take my yoke upon you and learn from me, for I am gentle and humble in heart, and you will find rest for your souls. For my yoke is easy and my burden is light' (Matthew 11:28–30, NIV).

Angela Griffiths is a member of the Association of Christian Writers and for four years was their official 'Encourager'. Her published work includes fiction and non-fiction for children, and prayers and devotional material for adults. She has also written nine books for young adults with reading difficulties.

An extract from (Extra)Ordinary Women

Clare Blake writes:

Have you ever felt that women in the Bible were super-stars, somehow extra specially blessed by God, and that this is why their names are recorded in scripture? 'Of course they must have had really special qualities for God to use them,' you might sigh. 'Not like me—I'm just ordinary.' But actually, when we look at these women more closely, we don't find this to be the case at all.

When I look at Martha complaining to Jesus that she's been left to do everything singlehanded and why doesn't Mary help—can't she see how much there is to do?—I get a sense of, 'Been there, done that!' Or what about the mother of James and John trying to get the best places in heaven for her sons? Have you ever wanted to push your kids into the limelight?

The more I look at these women, the more I realize that they experienced the same tensions, hopes and fears and struggled with the same universal feminine dilemmas as the rest of us. And if God can use a Mary or a Martha, a Sarah, a Leah or a Rebekah in all their human frailty, then what's to stop him using me?

God looks beyond our failings and weaknesses to the women we will become as we learn to follow him, step by faltering step. To him, each of us is a 'one off' with a unique combination of personality and giftings. In his eyes there are no 'ordinary' women—only 'extraordinary' women—and he loves us to bits!

Who, me, Lord?

It was just a normal day in Mary's home as she busied herself about her daily chores. Perhaps she was spinning, or baking bread for the evening meal. However, this was one day that Mary was never going to forget. Just having an angel appear was extraordinary enough. It certainly wasn't an everyday happening in the small town of Nazareth where she lived. She had never met anyone like him before. But when he spoke, what he said was even more surprising: 'Greetings, favoured one! The Lord is with you.'

Surely he couldn't mean her? She was just a humble village girl. 'Favoured one!' What did it all mean? Mary probably wondered at first whether there had been some mistake. 'Who, me, Lord?'

God delights in taking uncertain people who cannot believe they have been chosen—'Who, me, Lord?'—and transforming them into radical men and women of God.

It was God who found Gideon hiding from the Midianites, threshing wheat in a wine press, and said to him, 'The Lord is with you, you mighty warrior!' (Judges 6:12). At the time, Gideon must have felt embarrassed and confused. Here he was, skulking away in fear for his life. Nothing could be further from the behaviour of a mighty warrior. 'Who, me, Lord? No, you've got the wrong person!'

God makes no mistakes, however. He doesn't choose people according to worldly values. He doesn't really care whether you have good qualifications or none at all, whether you are rich and famous or poor and nondescript. He looks at your heart response to him, and very often it is those who are weakest in the world's eyes that he can use most because they realize how much they need to depend on him.

Paul reassures us in 1 Corinthians 1:26–27 that of those responding to God's call, 'not many of you were wise by human standards, not many were powerful, not many were of noble birth. But God chose what is foolish in the world to shame the wise; God chose what is weak in the world to shame the strong.'

When you look at the first followers of Jesus you realize what a motley crew they were. They included loud-mouthed Peter who was continually getting into hot water, a reformed prostitute and even a future traitor—not ideal candidates for the job!

All of these people probably thought when Jesus called them, 'Who, me, Lord? But you don't know what my life has been like. I've made so many mistakes. I'm really not worthy to be your follower at all!'

We can be just the same. We've probably all experienced the gentle prodding of the Holy Spirit to do something for Jesus: to talk to that other mum at the school gate, begin teaching a Sunday School group, pray out loud in the midweek meeting, or hold a coffee morning for Third World relief. The problem is that very often these things, small though they might seem in comparison to Gideon leading God's army or Moses' confrontations with Pharaoh (Exodus 5— 11), can have just as much power to make us shake in our shoes.

We may feel inadequate for the task ahead of us and may be tempted to argue with God. 'You want me to do this for you, Lord? Surely you don't mean me. I'd make a total mess of it! Why don't you choose Ruth or Jane or Grace? I'm sure they'd make a much better job of it. I'd only let you down.'

I hope we wouldn't get as far as employing Jonah's tactics. Jonah tried to run away from the task God gave him, and it took several days in the belly of a fish to bring him to his senses and convince him that the right course of action was to obey God.

Mary's response was totally different. Probably no one else has ever been given such an awesome task to fulfil—to be the mother of God's Son. Mary must have felt completely out of her depth. She wasn't even married and might have had to face the stigma of public disapproval and even the loss of her fiancé. Yet she was able to face the task before her with grace and joy, 'Here am I, the servant of the Lord; let it be with me according to your word' (Luke 1:38).

When God asks us to do something for him we may whisper faintheartedly, 'Who, me, Lord?' Jesus just looks at us with such love in his eyes. He knows exactly what we're like—all our strengths, our weaknesses, our worries, our fears. He knows us inside out, warts and all.

'Yes, you, daughter,' he replies. 'Come, follow me.'

Small cogs

Do you ever have the feeling that you are just a small cog in a very big wheel? Perhaps you are a mum with young children, who can't remember how it feels to be able to talk to friends for a solid hour without constant interruptions—nowadays you've almost forgotten how to string a sentence together! Or maybe you work in a place where job satisfaction is minimal and you feel undervalued as a person, just part of the office furniture.

The little maid in 2 Kings 5 was right at the bottom of the social pecking order of her time. In fact, she was so insignificant in the terms of her culture that we don't even know her name. All we know is that she had been captured as a young girl and taken away from her home in Israel. She was alone in a land whose ways were foreign to her. Her family was lost—almost certainly she would never see them again. Perhaps they had even been killed in the same raid when she was captured. She was no longer free to do what she wanted when she wanted. Instead she had to obey the commands of a master and a mistress and live surrounded by those who were enemies of her people. In fact, her master was not just anyone—he was one of the most brilliant military commanders on the opposite side.

He was also a very sick man, plagued with leprosy. The little maid had good cause to hate and fear him. He had taken her away from everything she loved. He was also an unbeliever—instead of the one true God, he worshipped heathen idols. How easy it would have been for the maid to become bitter and resentful in her captivity. Hadn't she lost everything?

There was one thing she hadn't lost, however. She still possessed the most important thing of all—her faith in God—and she knew that her God, the God of Israel, had the power to heal Naaman in his desperate need.

Many in her situation would have been tempted to withhold the information. Let Naaman ask the foreign gods he worshipped for help! Why should an enemy of Israel be saved? Let him suffer! The maid reacted differently. Despite her captivity, she had not become bitter and twisted. Although technically Naaman was the enemy, she reached out to him as another human being needing to know the sovereign love of God.

You can sense the quiet faith of this young girl as she speaks to her mistress. 'If only my lord were with the prophet who is in Samaria! He would cure him of his leprosy' (2 Kings 5:3). She had no doubt at all that the God in whom she trusted would heal Naaman.

I am sure that when Naaman's wife first told him what their serving maid had said, he was tempted to dismiss it. Wealthy and influential, he would certainly have spent time and money consulting the best doctors he could find. The little maid—she was a nobody! Why should he, the mighty Naaman, take her advice? But there must have been something in her that won him over. As she served them day after day in the most menial of tasks, something shone through that convinced him that this young woman knew what she was talking about, and made him prepared to take the step of trusting her.

In the eyes of Naaman's household, the maid was insignificant, but in God's eyes she had a key part to play. What would have happened if she had been so overawed by the high status of her employer that she hadn't dared to speak up and bring God's perspective? What if she'd thought, 'He's my boss—how can I possibly speak to him? He'll never listen to me!' The maid knew that position didn't matter. She knew that, far from being a nobody, she was a somebody because God loved her. She looked beyond the limitations of her circumstances and continued acting as a child of God in the situation in which she found herself.

Because of her obedience, Naaman, one of the greatest leaders in the land, did end up being healed; but more than this, he met with the living God in whom his servant believed and trusted, and his whole life was radically changed.

We should never feel disqualified from serving God by what we do. It really doesn't matter whether we hold an important position or whether in the world's eyes we are of no value at all, spending most of the day at the kitchen sink.

The fact is that God is with us wherever we are—at home, at work, in our leisure pursuits, in every moment of every day. Like the unnamed maid, we can allow God to work through us and change the lives of those around us.

You can find further details of this book on page 154, and an order form on page 157. Alternatively, (Extra)Ordinary Women is available from your local Christian bookshop.

Other Christina Press titles

Who'd Plant a Church? Diana Archer
£5.99 in UK
Planting an Anglican church from scratch, with a team of four—
two adults and two children—is an unusual adventure even in
these days. Diana Archer is a vicar's wife who gives a distinctive
perspective on parish life.

Pathway Through Grief edited by Jean Watson
£6.99 in UK
Ten Christians, each bereaved, share their experience of loss.
Frank and sensitive accounts offering comfort and reassurance
to those recently bereaved. Jean Watson has lost her own husband and believes that those involved in counselling will also
gain new insights from these honest personal chronicles.

God's Catalyst Rosemary Green
£8.99 in UK
Rosemary Green's international counselling ministry has prayer
and listening to God at its heart. Changed lives and rekindled
faith testify to God's healing power. Here she provides insight,
inspiration and advice for both counsellors and concerned
Christians who long to be channels of God's Spirit to help those
in need. God's Catalyst is a unique tool for the non-specialist
counsellor; for the pastor who has no training; for the Christian
who wants to come alongside hurting friends.

Angels Keep Watch Carol Hathorne
£5.99 in UK
A true adventure showing how God still directs our lives,not
with wind, earthquake or fire, but by the still, small voice.
  'Go to Africa.' The Lord had been saying it for over forty
years. At last, Carol Hathorne had obeyed, going out to Kenya
with her husband. On the eastern side of Nairobi, where tourists
never go, they came face to face with dangers, hardships and
poverty on a daily basis, but experienced the joy of learning that
Christianity is still growing in God's world.

Not a Super-Saint Liz Hansford
£6.99 in UK

'You might have thought Adrian Plass… had cornered the market in amusing diary writing. Well, check out Liz Hansford's often hilarious account of life as a Baptist minister's wife in Belfast. Highly recommended.' *The New Christian Herald*

Liz Hansford describes the outlandish situations which arise in the Manse, where life is both fraught and tremendous fun. *Not a Super-Saint* is for the ordinary Christian who feels they must be the only one who hasn't quite got it all together.

The Addiction of a Busy Life Edward England
£5.99 in UK

Twelve lessons from a devastating heart attack. Edward, a giant of Christian publishing in the UK, and founder of Christina Press, shares what the Lord taught him when his life nearly came to an abrupt end. Although not strictly a Christina title (Edward lacks the gender qualifications), we believe you may want to buy this for the busy men in your lives.

'A wonderful story of success and frailty, of love and suffering, of despair and hope. If you are too busy to read this book, you are too busy.' *Dr Michael Green*

Life Path Luci Shaw
£5.99 in UK

Personal and spiritual growth through journal writing. Life has a way of slipping out of the back door while we're not looking. Keeping a journal can enrich life as we live it, and bring it all back later. Luci Shaw shows how a journal can also help us grow in our walk with God.

Precious to God Sarah Bowen
£5.99 in UK

Two young people, delighted to be starting a family, have their expectations shattered by the arrival of a handicapped child. And yet this is only the first of many difficulties to be faced. What was initially a tragedy is, through faith, transformed into a story of inspiration, hope and spiritual enrichment.

All the above titles are available from Christian bookshops everywhere, or in case of difficulty, direct from Christina Press using the order form on page 156.

Other BRF titles

(Extra)Ordinary Women Clare Blake
Reflections for women on Bible-based living
£6.99 in UK

Have you ever felt that women in the Bible were superstars, somehow extra specially blessed by God? And then looked at yourself…?

This book of down-to-earth Bible reflections is based around the central theme that all women are special in God's eyes. Relating Scripture teaching to everday experience, it shows how God has a special gifting for each of us, how we can turn to him when life doesn't make sense, and how to set about discovering his will for our lives.

Taking a fresh look at the stories of Sarah, Leah, Mary, and other Bible characters, we see how God looks beyond our failures and weaknesses to the women he has created us to be as we learn to follow him, step by step

'This is a book to dip into, to take on a weekend away, to keep in your bag or at your bedside. It will also be a treasure to give to your friends.' (Wendy Virgo)

The Song of Hope Judith Pinhey
Psalms and meditations for today
£6.99 in UK

The song of hope is a song we can sing even when we look at the pain and destruction which are all too real in the natural world and in our lives… Christian hope is a firm hope because it depends not on our human nature or circumstances, nor on the avoidance of the harshness of reality, but on God's love.

These new psalms and meditations can be used for private reading and reflection, or read aloud as part of group worship and prayer. Arranged in sections named after the four seasons, they also echo the themes and images of the Church's year, seeking to bring us to fresh wonder at the grace and mercy of God.

A Time to Wait Liz Morris
Bible insights on trusting God's timing
£3.99 in UK

In today's 'instant access' culture, the idea of waiting seems irrelevant, outdated. People like fast cars, fast food, money at the touch of a button. Every part of life is caught up in the rush, with even Christians developing a taste for faith geared to quick answers, problem-solving, and miracles on demand.

So what happens when we find God asking us to wait?

This is a book for everybody who is trying to live according to God's timing—perhaps reluctantly! It is for those who may fear that God has even forgotten them, despite the promises he gives through the Bible. Reflecting on some familiar Bible stories and characters, Liz Morris sets out some of the lessons that can help us along the way.

'We are indebted to Liz for sharing her insights with such wisdom and love.' (Faith Forster)

Still Time for Eternity Margaret Cundiff
£6.99 in UK

In the midst of our busyness, and the even greater rush of the wider world, there are few times when we stand still long enough to see the big picture, the working of God's kingdom values here on earth.

Taking a series of 'snapshots' over time from the winding up of the last century and the beginning of this one, Margaret Cundiff reflects on how we can discover God's love and concern in action. She brings together reflections on Scripture with events in everyday life, as well as in the newspapers and TV bulletins. What we find is that these moments, captured in the heart for whatever reason, are worth a second look before we all dash on. After all, there is still time for eternity—and that's what really matters.

All the above titles are available from Christian bookshops everywhere or, in case of difficulty, direct from BRF using the order form on page 157.

Christina Press Publications Order Form

All of these publications are available from Christian bookshops everywhere or, in case of difficulty, direct from the publisher. Please make your selection below, complete the payment details and send your order with payment as appropriate to:

Christina Press Ltd, 17 Church Road, Tunbridge Wells, Kent TN1 1LG

		Qty	Price	Total
8700	God's Catalyst	___	£8.99	___
8702	Precious to God	___	£5.99	___
8703	Angels Keep Watch	___	£5.99	___
8704	Life Path	___	£5.99	___
8705	Pathway Through Grief	___	£6.99	___
8706	Who'd Plant a Church?	___	£5.99	___
8708	Not a Super-Saint	___	£6.99	___
8705	The Addiction of a Busy Life	___	£5.99	___

POSTAGE AND PACKING CHARGES				
	UK	Europe	Surface	Air Mail
£7.00 & under	£1.25	£2.25	£2.25	£3.50
£7.10–£29.99	£2.25	£5.50	£7.50	£11.00
£30.00 & over	free	prices on request		

Total cost of books   £ _____
Postage and Packing   £ _____
TOTAL   £ _____

All prices are correct at time of going to press, are subject to the prevailing rate of VAT and may be subject to change without prior warning.

Name _____

Address _____

_____

_____ Postcode _____

Total enclosed £ _____ (cheques should be made payable to 'Christina Press Ltd')

◻ Please send me further information about Christina Press publications

BRF Publications Order Form

All of these publications are available from Christian bookshops everywhere, or in case of difficulty direct from the publisher. Please make your selection below, complete the payment details and send your order with payment as appropriate to:

BRF, First Floor, Elsfield Hall, 15–17 Elsfield Way, Oxford OX2 8FG

		Qty	Price	Total
235 1	(Extra)Ordinary Women	____	£6.99	____
261 0	The Song of Hope	____	£6.99	____
048 0	A Time to Wait	____	£3.99	____
212 2	Still Time for Eternity	____	£6.99	____

POSTAGE AND PACKING CHARGES				
	UK	Europe	Surface	Air Mail
£7.00 & under	£1.25	£3.00	£3.50	£5.50
£7.10–£29.99	£2.25	£5.50	£6.50	£10.00
£30.00 & over	free	prices on request		

Total cost of books   £ ____

Postage and Packing   £ ____

TOTAL   £ ____

All prices are correct at time of going to press, are subject to the prevailing rate of VAT and may be subject to change without prior warning.

Name _____

Address _____

_____ Postcode _____

Total enclosed £ _____ (cheques should be made payable to 'BRF')
Payment by: cheque ❑ postal order ❑ Visa ❑ Mastercard ❑ Switch ❑

Card no. ⬚⬚⬚⬚⬚⬚⬚⬚⬚⬚⬚⬚⬚⬚⬚⬚⬚⬚⬚

Card expiry date ⬚⬚⬚⬚   Issue number (Switch) ⬚⬚⬚⬚

Signature _____

(essential if paying by credit/Switch card)

❑ Please do not send me further information about BRF publications

Visit the BRF website at www.brf.org.uk

DBDWGMay03   BRF is a Registered Charity

Subscription Information

Each issue of *Day by Day with God* is available from Christian book-shops everywhere. Copies may also be available through your church Book Agent or from the person who distributes Bible reading notes in your church.

Alternatively you may obtain *Day by Day with God* on subscription direct from the publishers. There are two kinds of subscription:

Individual Subscriptions are for four copies or less, and include postage and packing. To order an annual Individual Subscription please complete the details on page 160 and send the coupon with payment to BRF in Oxford. You can also use the form to order a Gift Subscription for a friend.

Church Subscriptions are for five copies or more, sent to one address, and are supplied post free. Church Subscriptions run from 1 May to 30 April each year and are invoiced annually. To order a Church Subscription please complete the details opposite and send the coupon to BRF in Oxford. You will receive an invoice with the first issue of notes.

All subscription enquiries should be directed to:

BRF
First Floor
Elsfield Hall
15–17 Elsfield Way
Oxford
OX2 8FG

Tel: 01865 319700
Fax: 01865 319701
E-mail: subscriptions@brf.org.uk